PUGET SOUNDS

A Nostalgic Review of Radio and
TV in the Great Northwest

PUGET SOUNDS

A Nostalgic Review of Radio and TV in the Great Northwest

DAVID RICHARDSON

 Superior Publishers
P.O. Box 1710, Seattle, WA. 98111

←
A local boy making good. **Bing Crosby** of Tacoma and Spokane in an early appearance. Photo courtesy of Kathryn Crosby.

Library of Congress Cataloging in Publication Data

Richardson, David Blair, 1926-
  Puget Sounds.

  Includes index.
  SUMMARY: Recalls moments in the origins of radio and television focusing particularly on the broadcasting history of Washington State.
  1. Broadcasting—Washington (State)—Puget Sound area—History.   [1. Broadcasting—Washington (State) —Puget Sound area—History]   I. Title.

PN1990.6.P84R5   791.44'09797'7   80-26557

ISBN 0-87564-636-0

FIRST EDITION

To the Northwest's Pioneers
of Wireless
and the "Visible Telephone"

Thanks to:

Susan Jones Abbott
Helen Sanislo Anderson
Bill Apple
Michael Bader
Shirley Bartholomew
Tom Bean
Len Beardsley
Leo Beckley
Rod Belcher
Ruth Bennett
Paul Benton
Don Bevilacqua
Galen Biery
Jeanne Boardman
John Boor
Stan Boreson
Mari Brattain
Syd Brockman
Gerald Brott
Elliott Brown
Tom Brown
Warren Brown
Bill Brubaker
Dorothy Bullitt
Neil Burmeister
Bruce Calhoun
Stan Carlson

Claire Chevigny
Ron Ciro
Jack Clarke
Wayne Cody
Les Cole
Lloyd Cooney
Joe Coscarart
Danny Coulthurst
Paul Crittenden
Dave Crockett
Kathryn Crosby
Tom Dargan
John Darwin Davis, Jr.
Robert Dietsch
Ivan Ditmars
John Dubuque
Don Duncan
Tom Duncan
Mercedes Edgerton
Fred Elsethagen
Jeanne Engerman
Bill Evans
Trevor Evans
Haines Fay
Hugh Feltis
Ken Fisher
Mrs. Harry Foster

Nick Foster
Ruth Fratt
Din Fuhrmeister
Mary Weller Fuller
Bob Galvin
Gwyneth Gamble
H. C. "Hap" Garthright
Marie Garthright
Jerry Geehan
Art Gilmore
Bob Gleason
Fred Goddard
Don Godfrey
Lyle Goltz
Tom Griffith
Nancy Gullick
Mrs. Saul Haas
Ivar Haglund
Agnes Hagman
Lola Hallowell
Ernie Harper
Marlowe Hartung
Christie Keplinger Hasson
Tom Haveman
Mrs. Carl Haymond

$\longrightarrow$

Thanks to (cont'd):

C. Dexter Haymond
Tom Herbert
Paul Herbold
Charles Herring
Len Higgins
Steven Hill
Vernice Irwin
Don Isham
Frank Jank
Bill Johnson
Dorothy Johnson
Harry Jordan
Mrs. Oscar Jorgenson
Ken Kager
Larry Kiner
Ted Knightlinger
Joe Kolesar
Bob Koons
Howard Kraft
Texas Jim Lewis
Beth Lyman
Pete Lyman
Bert McAllister
Bill McLain
Morgan McMahon
Erling Manley
Grant Merrill
Dave Mintz
Jim Moore
Harold Morrill

Charles Morris
Paul Morris
Julie Moser
H. Ben Murphy
Virginia Hesketh Murray
Jim Neidigh
Mary Lee Nichols
Wendell Niles
Ham O'Hara
Ancel Payne
George Peckham
Alton Phillips
Bill Pickering
Homer Pope
John Price
Bob Priebe
Ruth Prins
Gil Reeves
Earl Reilly
Bill Reuter
Mrs. Paul Rhymer
Virginia Riley
Ken Ritchie
Al Roberts
Jim Ross
Lanny Ross
Hugh Rundell
Beverly Russell
Milo Ryan
Robert Sanislo
Rosalie Sayyah

Lee Schulman
Al Schuss
Ben Sefrit
Jack Shawcroft
Marian Simpson
Al Smith
Thomas Freebairn Smith
Bob Spence
Loren Stone
Ken Stuart, Jr.
Mary Suder
Norrie Suder
Al Swift
Elsie Swisher
Earl Thoms
Gordon Thorne
Gary Tubesing
Gordon Tuell
Jim Upthegrove
Edo Vanni
Elmore Vincent
Robert Vrooman
Al Wallace
Florence Wasmer
Gene Wecker
Dick Weeks
Woodrow Wells
Bob Wikstrom
Hal Willard
Charles Williams
Norma Zimmer

And to:

CBS, IGM, KCBS, KCTS, KDKA, KGMI, KING, KIRO, KJR, KOMO, KRKO, KSTW, KVOS, RCA, WGY, WWJ; Communications Satellite Corp. (COMSAT); the Magnavox Consumer Electronics Co.; the 3M Co., Manufacturers of "Scotch" Recording Tape; The Fisher Companies; and the Seattle chapters of the American Federation of Television and Radio Artists, and the National Academy of Television Arts and Sciences; for the use of pictures.

The Broadcast Pioneers Library, Washington, D.C.; the Crosby Library, Gonzaga University, Spokane; the Kentucky Historical Society; the National Archives, Seattle and Washington, D.C.; the Smithsonian Institution; St. Martin's Abbey, Lacey, Wash.; the Seattle Historical Society's Museum of History and Industry; the Seattle Public Library; the Tacoma Public Library's Marvin D. Boland Photograph Collection; the Northwest, Manuscript, and Photography Collections in the Suzzallo Library, the University of Washington, Seattle; the Washington State Library, Olympia; the Washington State Historical Society Museum, Tacoma; and the Whatcom Museum of History and Art, Bellingham; for information and pictures.

The Seattle Post-Intelligencer, Seattle Times, and Tacoma News Tribune; for the use of photographs.

Bill Brubaker, KOMO; for four photographs of KFQX.

Broadcasting Magazine; for permission to reproduce two cartoons by Sid Hix.

Photographers Art Forde and Fred Milkie; for permission to use pictures of theirs.

Larry Hoffman and Willard Stone; for expert copying and restoring of old photographs.

All of you in broadcasting whose pictures I didn't use (or couldn't find) and whose anecdotes and histories (though fascinating) I was unable to include; for understanding.

CONTENTS

CHAPTER ONE
The Attic of the Mind   9

CHAPTER TWO
Sounds from a Box   15

CHAPTER THREE
Aunt Vivian   26

CHAPTER FOUR
"Blend's Mah Friend"   40

CHAPTER FIVE
Pioneers and G-Men   57

CHAPTER SIX
"The Friendly Station"   68

CHAPTER SEVEN
KING's Kameras   89

CHAPTER EIGHT
"The Naked Truth"   112

CHAPTER NINE
"The Musical Station"   133

CHAPTER TEN
Mr. Baseball   151

CHAPTER ELEVEN
"The Voice of Seattle"   168

CHAPTER TWELVE
Stay Tuned for Tomorrow   182

APPENDIX   187

INDEX   190

Stan Boreson entertained with music and fun over **KING-TV** weekday afternoons for 18 years. When the happy Scandinavian began the show in 1949, television—like Stan's lethargic basset hound "No Mo Shun"—was merely a pup.

CHAPTER ONE

The Attic of the Mind

This is a memory book, not a history book.

A sentimental ramble back into time, back, back to our youth and childhood and before. Back to the magic that was radio and the ghostly flicker of that first 8-inch TV.

Remember?

Wunda Wunda, pretty lady in a clown suit, creating misty castles of enchantment.

"Heavenly days, McGee, don't open that closet!"

"Zero dachus, Mucho Crackus, Hallaballooza Bub." Now we're all lifetime members of lutefisk-voiced Stan Boreson's zany club.

Gildersleeve's horsey laugh. The Kingfish selling gullible Andy on another scheme. "Hi-yo, Silver!" Say, who was that masked man, anyway?

Brakeman Bill tootling the "Cartoon Special" down the O-gauge track, or trading quips with Crazy Donkey. J. P. Patches celebrating his birthday—on April Fool's day, of course.

Or this:

The voice is high pitched and raspy as a raven's croak. "It's a high fly ball to the left field wall! Back, back, back, back, back—and it's *overrrr*!" It's Leo Lassen, "Mr. Baseball," bringing his special magic to the game once again.

If you're *really* an old-timer, you remember winding your own coil on a round Quaker Oats box. Fiddling with the crystal and cat's whisker, trying to hear the "A & P Gypsies." Grandpa, with earphones on, his eyes suddenly alight: "Hey, everybody, I got Spokane!"

Or "Aunt Vivian's" fishy bedtime yarns.

Or the "Hoot Owls" from Portland.

It's hard for today's generations to imagine the awesome impact of radio's arrival in the twenties. To sit at home and hear a sound, a voice, a song, from clear across town—even from some far distant city one had heard about, but never seen, and likely never would see—without intervening wires! It was the new century's ultimate miracle.

Newspapers ran daily columns trying to explain how radio works. Whole pages were devoted to the letters and telegrams sent in by "radiophans" describing their reception of local and distant stations.

The papers also ran advance notice of music to be played on the air, even to specific phonograph records. In 1922 you might have heard Alma Gluck sing "Lo, Hear the Gentle Lark," or the "Southern Rose Waltz" by Guatemala's Royal Marimba Band. Quite different fare from that offered by the same station, KJR, these days.

Not everyone approved of radio. Some people were sure it was bad for the ears. Others feared that radio sets might attract "stray electricity" and start fires.

Yet the manufacturers of receivers and parts couldn't turn them out fast enough. Seattle's Kilbourne & Clark, with 75 employes, was in a frenzy. Dealers would come by, clamoring to have backlogs of orders filled. Finally they just had to roll up their sleeves and help assemble their own sets.

Crystal sets gave way to multistage tube receivers. Some of them had so many knobs it took an engineer to tune one properly. And if you did it wrong, your receiver became a transmitter and blanked out your neighbors' reception.

Everybody thought television was just around the corner. A story in the P-I predicted $150 TV sets "in every home by the end of next year," enabling "wives to check up on telephone messages from husbands detained in the office."

That was in 1927.

With the advent of network hookups and "remote control" broadcasts, many new careers were launched. Everybody knows Tacoma-born Bing Crosby got his first big break on the road with Paul Whiteman's orchestra. Not everyone realizes Bing bombed in New York, got arrested in L. A. and was fired in Seattle.

He was just another singer when he got back to Hollywood and signed on with Gus Arnheim's band at the Coconut Grove.

But Arnheim was doing a nightly dance remote on a West Coast radio hookup. Bing's "boo-boo-boo" crooning style caught on with the listeners and suddenly he was famous. Even in the Midwest people were

sitting up till three a.m. to catch him. A year later Bill Paley of CBS gave him his first national radio show, for Cremo cigars.

Network programs were always live, and there were three hours' difference between East and West Coasts. So the big-name performers all did their shows twice. Somehow the West Coast repeat was much more interesting. Maybe because the stars would kill the two hours between shows at a nearby bar.

Radio sold ads to keep its pot boiling, and not everyone was happy about that. Lee De Forest, the inventor, cried in earnest (but vain) protest against "the crass commercialism, the etheric vandalism of the vulgar hucksters, agencies, advertisers, station owners —all who, lacking awareness of their grand opportunities and moral responsibilities to make of radio an uplifting influence, continue to enslave and sell for quick cash the grandest medium which has yet been given to man. . . ."

Ruth Prins as "Wunda Wunda," every child's favorite story-lady.

Yet broadcasting served us well. Radio drama, the "theater of the mind," entertained us nightly. We laughed with the great comics, cried with the soap opera heroines, were sobered by ghostly short-wave voices threatening war.

The Depression was on but we heard F.D.R. saying all we had to fear was fear itself, and his reassuring voice from the White House fireside helped hold the nation together.

Then came the "day that will live in infamy," and we marched off to war—or stayed home and listened as a local boy named Ed Murrow told us all about it.

Finally TV came along and we all learned a new vocabulary. Video, test pattern, Yagi antenna, fine tuning. Uncle Miltie, Mr. Peepers, and Kukla, Fran and Ollie. The Slo-Mo's and No-Mo and rooster tail fever. "Sheriff" Tex and Captain Puget.

The Vast Wasteland.

Not everyone approved of television. They thought it was bad for the eyes and might give everyone cancer.

But in darkened living rooms the ectoplasmic blue light glowed and we watched Morey Amsterdam and Sid Caesar and Lucy and more old movies than you can shake a TV dinner at. Funny how many friends you suddenly had, if your ten-inch set was the first on the block. Later, everyone had one, and all over town the toilets flushed in unison when the commercial came along.

Joe Towey, lugubrious host of **KIRO-TV**'s midnight horror movies on "Nightmare Theater."

Chris Wedes as "J. P. Patches" and **Bob Newman** as "Gertrude" on **KIRO-TV**'s popular kids' show.

11

"And now get ready to smile again with radio's home-folks, Vic and Sade...." Over 30 years since its last broadcast, the whimsical daytime show written by **Paul Rhymer** still has an active fan club. (See Appendix.)

Seated, from left: **Art Van Harvey** (Vic), **Bernadine Flynn** (Sade), **Paul Rhymer**, actor **Walter Huston** and poet **Edgar Guest**. Standing: unidentified NBC producer and **William Idelson** (Rush).

Comedian **Jack Benny** and Seattle-born **Mary Livingstone**, whose real name was Sadie Marks. The first time they met she was only 12; Jack was dating her sister. Years later they became reacquainted in Los Angeles, and yes, their running gag was true: she was a hosiery clerk for the May Co. store while Jack courted her.

They were married in 1927. Benny was traveling the vaudeville circuit, his first radio appearance (on "The Ed Sullivan Show") still four years away. His own show debuted on CBS in 1932. "The Jack Benny Program" with Mary and such other regulars as Don Wilson, Phil Harris, Dennis Day, "Rochester" (Eddie Anderson) and the multi-voiced Mel Blanc was a hit through all of radio's golden period and the early years of TV.

Elizabeth Leonard (left) and **Casey Gregarson** on KING-TV's long-running daytime program "Telescope."

"Brakeman Bill" (**Bill McLain**) and admirers, about 1956, on Channel 11.

Broadcasting is a part of our lives now, and will be. Every today holds a wealth of excitement for eye or ear, while the tomorrows all promise new surprises and delights.

Meanwhile the yesterdays occupy a special place in our hearts. Nostalgia for "Old Time Radio" is epidemic. Anyone with a tape machine or record player can hear the old programs all over again. Hundreds, if not thousands of North Americans collect tapes of shows from radio's golden era. Dozens or hundreds go around ransacking attics and basements for vintage Philcos and Gilfillans and Atwater Kents to restore to perfect playing condition. Scores of publications are devoted to these hobbies, and to the collectors of related memorabilia—decoder pins, photos, rings, buttons, shaker mugs and all the other premiums we used to save our dimes and box tops for.

(A number of addresses where readers can get in touch will be found in the Appendix.)

Meanwhile we have assembled our own treasure of radio and TV lore from the archives, attics and memories of Puget Sound area stations and broadcasters and other sources. So return with us now to those exciting days of yesteryear! From out of the past come the half-forgotten voices and images that so thrilled us before. Let them thrill us again in nostalgic retrospect.

Your seat is reserved, front row center.

The house lights dim; the curtain rises.

And here is the first act.

Weather forecaster **Ray Ramsey**, anchorman **Bill Brubaker** and sportscaster **Bruce King** of the "**KOMO** News 4" team.

Brubaker, while a University of Washington graduate student, unearthed much early history of Puget Sound area broadcasting to gain a Master's Degree in Communications. His thesis forms an obvious starting point for researching this or any other book on the subject.

CHAPTER TWO

Sounds from a Box

Who invented radio?

Ah, that is a question. Italy's Guglielmo Marconi leaps most readily to mind, perhaps. But Russia honors its Alexander Popov, Germany recognizes Heinrich Hertz, and Canadians credit their Reginald Fessenden. Actually, strong evidence suggests the *real* father of radio—are you ready for this?—was an eccentric Kentucky truck farmer named Nathan Stubblefield.

Inventions rarely pop full-blown, of course, like a cartoonist's light bulb, from a single fertile mind. Politics, money, and the fickle finger of fate all play their role.

America's Benjamin Franklin made the basic discovery: that an electric current will follow a wire, even a very long one, back to its source. For decades afterward, scientists wrestled to turn this fact into a long-distance signalling device. In their laboratories they could swing pith balls, ring bells and magnetize needles, but they couldn't figure out how to send messages without using 26 separate wires: one for each letter of the alphabet.

Samuel F. B. Morse was no scientist, and never really understood much about electricity. He earned his living painting portraits. But whiling away the long days of an ocean voyage he conceived the dots and dashes of Morse code, and the electric telegraph was born.

Now the race was on to figure how to transmit the human voice itself. Contenders borrowed or stole one another's ideas and it looked like a dead heat to the finish line. Alexander Graham Bell beat his nearest rival, Elisha Gray, to the patent office by just two hours.

Two hours more, and we'd be cussing out Ma Gray and the Gray System today.

At that, Bell cheated a little. Because he hadn't actually built a working telephone yet, and didn't really know if the device he had in mind would work or not. Now to find out. With trembling hands he poured acid into the gadget he called a transmitter, spilling some on his pants. His first words into the device were to his surprised assistant in another room: "Mr. Watson, come here! I want you!"

Bell, you see, was a Scotsman. Just then he was more concerned about saving his trousers than making history.

Pioneer telegraphers had observed a fascinating thing. The dots and dashes racing over their wires produced strange phenomena, like deflecting compass needles, at considerable distances away from the lines themselves. And when the first phone service began in London, subscribers complained of picking up a constant click-click from the city's telegraph circuits. Some visionaries concluded there must be a way to send messages without using wires at all.

Heinrich Hertz doped out the theory of wireless waves in his laboratory, and tinkerers in a dozen lands started the search for a way to put his ideas to practice. The most determined of these hopefuls was the Irish-Italian teenager, Guglielmo (William) Marconi.

Fortunately, Bill had an indulgent and well heeled father to bankroll his experiments with coils, spark gaps and other mysterious paraphernalia strung between the peas and cabbages of the family farm. In two years, Marconi had devised apparatus that could send and receive messages for more than a mile. With this he stormed England, where awed financiers set up a company enabling him to build more powerful equipment.

Soon Marconi stations were bridging rugged coastlines and saving lives at sea. Then, on December 12, 1901, the first weak, rasping notes were exchanged between Poldhu, in England, and St. John's, Newfoundland. The prearranged signals were a mere three dots—Morse code for "s"—repeated over and over. But Marconi heard them.

Wireless had conquered the Atlantic Ocean.

Guglielmo Marconi pictured with primitive receiving equipment being installed at St. John's, Newfoundland, Dec. 12, 1901. Nine days later Marconi picked up history's first transatlantic wireless signals, transmitted from Marconi's station at Poldhu, on the Cornish coast of England.

Nathan B. Stubblefield, reputed inventor of the radiotelephone. Stubblefield's apparatus was crude, and worked over a very short range; but he appears to have achieved the wireless transmission of voice and music long before anyone else.

The next step was obvious: modulate the Marconi signal, as Bell had done with Morse's telegraph, to achieve a wireless telephone. But it wasn't all that easy. Telegraph signals need only a relatively small electric current to work. To reach useful levels of wireless energy, antenna currents of a much higher order are required. Nevertheless, many hopefuls tried coupling a Bell microphone directly to their power supply or antenna. No more danger to their clothes—carbon granules had long since replaced the dangerous sulphuric acid.

But a good many lips were scorched in these experiments with "hot" microphones!

Yet some backyard tinkerers did produce apparatus that would work over modest distances. And the first to succeed seems to have been the gaunt mystery man from Murray, Kentucky, Nathan B. Stubblefield.

On New Year's Day, 1903—not three weeks after Marconi's signals first spanned the ocean—Stubblefield came out from behind the high, untrimmed hedge surrounding his home and farmyard. A thousand townspeople gathered with reporters in front of the courthouse and there he demonstrated his wireless phone. He spoke into the microphone and was heard clearly in a receiver at the far end of the square. His son Bernard even played a harmonica solo into the device—perhaps the first musical "broadcast" in history.

Mr. and Mrs. Nathan B. Stubblefield and children at their home in Murray, Kentucky. At the extreme left is **Bernard**, the son who helped Stubblefield with his experiments. Not long after this photo was taken, the Stubblefields separated. Nathan, who had hoped to make millions, subsequently starved to death.

In March, 1902 Stubblefield took his equipment to Washington and made a demonstration to government and business leaders, broadcasting from the deck of the steamer *Bartholdi* on the Potomac River. The experiment was a technical success, but a promotional failure. Broken and embittered, Stubblefield returned to Kentucky and lived in seclusion, unrecognized and impoverished. He died in 1928. Decades later an act of Kentucky's legislature has proclaimed him the true "Father of Radio."

Then Stubblefield packed his equipment into an ordinary country store soda keg and traveled with it to Washington and Philadelphia, where he must have supposed business and government men would smother him with money and honors. It didn't happen. When the shy Kentuckian returned to Murray he was a broken man, both financially and in spirit. His wife left him. His home was sold to pay creditors. He retired to a tiny dirt-floor shack built of tin and cornstalks, and eventually died there, a bitter and penniless recluse.

But wait!

The most fascinating thing of all about Nathan Stubblefield is the claim that he had actually invented the wireless telephone by 1892—*or even earlier!* In other words, five years or more before Marconi began experimenting with dots and dashes, the lone inventor of Murray, Kentucky had made a quantum leap and was sending human voices through the air.

A tall tale? Perhaps, but for the positive testimony of an eyewitness who saw the apparatus in action. And that witness was one of Murray's most respected citizens, an attorney and founder of the state university which today occupies the site of Stubblefield's old farm.

Other inventors were more successful at promoting themselves and their discoveries. One was Canadian-born Professor Reginald Fessenden, whose backers included two Pittsburgh, Pennsylvania millionaires. With money no particular object, Fessenden constructed a large experimental station at Brant Rock, on the Massachusetts coast. He ordered special equipment built to his design, including a one-kilowatt alternator and a water-cooled, asbestos-cased microphone. By Christmas Eve, 1906, the hookup was ready for a test.

That night, wireless operators on ships off the New England coast were stunned to hear crackling through their earphones not the crashing, raspy di-dahs of Morse code, but the calm, unmistakable tones of a man's voice speaking to them. Then a woman's sweet soprano notes came to them in song, and after that a violin played "O, Holy Night."

By now the wireless rooms were crowded. Officers and sailors listened, hardly believing, as the man read them verses from the Gospel of St. Luke, and concluded the test with wishes for a Merry Christmas.

The man who spoke to them, and played his violin, was Professor Fessenden. The soprano solo came from a phonograph, pushed up close to the microphone. Not every word and note came through clearly. The equipment was primitive. The signal was weak, and sounded hollow.

But it was a kind of miracle all the same. Broadcasting was really born that Christmas Eve in 1906, off the coast of Massachusetts.

THE SEATTLE SUNDAY TIMES, OCT. 30, 1910.

SEATTLE BOY TAKES WORLD RECOR

Invents Wireless Telephone That Reaches Tacon

MORAN SHIPYARD SITE PURCHASED FOR $2,500,000

A. Murray, President of American Savings Bank & Trust Company, Obtains Control of Fine Property.

TO SPEND MILLIONS UPON IMPROVEMENTS

Understood Marine Concern Will Remain on Ground It Uses at Present Time for Indeterminate Period.

FOR a consideration upwards of $2,500,000, James A. Murray, president of the American Savings Bank & Trust company has purchased the site of the Moran Company's ship yards that have been closed (John in New York. By the terms of the transfer the Moran ship yards will remain on the premises for an indeterminate period.

Half of the property not now in use for ship building purposes probably will be improved by Mr. Murray, at a cost of more than $2,000,000, making his total investment in the new deal nearly, if not quite, $5,000,000.

Already Largely Interested.

Mr. Murray is now in New York. He is president and controlling owner in the Meridian Trust Company, which owns two double corners at Third Avenue and Union Street, as well as the site of the Arctic Club Building. Mr. Murray is interested in Seattle prior to his last purchase have been in excess of $2,000,000, and he is president and chief stockholder in the American Savings Bank & Trust Company, at Second Avenue and Madison Street.

Business associates of Mr. Murray, who is a retired Montana millionaire, now living at Monterey, Cal., confirmed yesterday to discuss his latest investment in Seattle. Marcus M. Murray, his nephew, who is cashier of the American Savings Bank & Trust Company, declared last night that he knew nothing of his own knowledge concerning the transaction.

ENEMIES OF GILL STULTIFY SELVES TO KNOCK MAYOR

In Mad Efforts to Injure Administration, Men Who Attack City Lighting Plant Strike Own Constituents.

EXECUTIVE FAITHFULLY CARRIED OUT PLEDGES

Gives Cheap Service to Annexed District, and Now Faces Bitter Assault for Being Honest With People.

THE fight against Mayor H. C. Gill and his administration has taken a new turn and the interests of suburban residents who were induced to vote for annexation on the ground that they would be given electric light and city water, have been attacked.

Something to St. Anne of the city lighting plant who is faithfully carrying out campaign pledges of Mayor Gill, the antagonistic prejudice of Seattle commercial bodies and the council's instructions, extending the city lighting facilities to the suburbs, has been made by the council showed its good faith by authorizing the extensions. In Mayor Gill's campaign for election, he told the people of the district lying north of the canal, in the Rainier Valley and West Seattle that he would push the extension of the city lighting plant for their benefit.

Relief From Monopoly Insistent.

He promised that he would advocate

Inventor Using His Wireless Telephone

William Dubilier, young inventor of wonderful instrument, at Seattle test station, talking to Tacoma.

WIZARD YOUTH PLUCKS VOIC FROM TH

Seattle May Be Made by Astounding Succ Young William Dubili Wireless Telephony.

BIG FACTORY TO MAH INSTRUMENTS PL

Triumph Crowns Car most as Romantic a usual as That of Gre ures of Lincoln's Per

This same button that tur electric lights in one office soon will operat cordially complex mechanism, not only to thos offices and homes but alsos its will eventually be introduc plate of a group of Seattl have incorporated the Comm less Telephone Manufacturin with a capital of $100,000 A site on which to erect is being sought to place the first factory of its kin world.

Tests during the past wee established a world's long dist call for wireless telephon of the most remarkable fe of the year, and William Dubilier, the Seventeen-ye old man, has established a wire phone communication with t phone communication with t not ten by ten inches, with six inches apparatus that 3ms phones placed on ear set, and on the entire number will through the workings of the apparatus.

Heard At Navy Yard

J. B. Annis, first class ele S. Signal Corps, at Bremerton Thursday night sent the young by Mr. Dubilier, following test of the wireless telephon

CITIZENS CLAIM

FATHER TIME'S

RIOTING FOLLOWS

ROOSEVELT CITES

(Seattle Times)

Paul J. Hackett reminisces about his early days as a radio experimenter in Seattle. With inventor William Dubilier, he developed a working radiotelephone transmitter set more than a half century before this 1968 photo was taken. Two of the devices were built, of which one was reportedly sold to the Russian government. The second, pictured here, now reposes in Seattle's Museum of History and Industry.

Across the nation, in Seattle, the American Telephone and Telegraph Company was looking for an engineer—someone familiar with the new technology of wireless. They settled on a brilliant nineteen-year-old New Yorker named William Dubilier. He came to Seattle in 1907, and immediately began devoting his spare time to experiments in wireless telephony.

Within two years, thousands of visitors to the big Alaska-Yukon-Pacific exposition, on grounds that are now the campus of the University of Washington, could see a crude demonstration of one short-range outfit. The following summer, 1910, Dubilier displayed his apparatus at Seattle's annual "Potlatch" celebration. Then in October, this "wizard youth"—as the Seattle Times was calling him—made national headlines by transmitting voice messages successfully from Seattle to Bremerton and Tacoma.

There was excited talk about building the world's first wireless telephone factory on Puget Sound. Half a million dollars were already subscribed. Seattle was to be the wireless phone capital of the world!

But the great factory was never built.* Dubilier's inventions were not really breakthroughs in wireless technology, but mere refinements of the still primitive "brute force method" of Professor Fessenden's day. Radio was still just a whisper, perilously riding bareback on an untamed thunderbolt.

The device that changed everything was the vacuum tube.

Actually, the tube had been kicking around as a laboratory curiosity for years. But nobody quite knew what to do with it. Then a genius named Lee De Forest added to its innards a few cents' worth of wire mesh he called a "control grid," and the age of electronics was born.

That bit of wire was to totally revolutionize transmitter and receiver circuits. Not to mention paving the way for such future wonders as record players, talking pictures, long distance telephone calls and TV sets. For now the weakest whisper, when applied to De Forest's grid, could be transformed into a powerful giant, faithfully shaping the mightiest electric currents to its precise will.

---

* Instead, Dubilier founded the Dubilier Condenser Co., an important manufacturer of radio parts.

A "musical trolley car" on the Seattle-Tacoma interurban line, about 1915. Experimenter Paul Hackett, working in Kent Valley with an arc transmitter and powerful microphone, discovered his signals were modulating the nearby trolley line's power system. Arc lamps on the cars acted like receivers and reproduced Hackett's music and voice transmissions, to the delight of riders. (Photo by Asahel Curtis.)

One of the tests was also picked up by an electric heater in the home of a woman who happened to know Hackett. Recognizing his voice, the startled lady was sure the inventor was hiding under her bed.

Dr. Lee De Forest with improved radiotelephone transmitter, about 1919. De Forest's development of the three-element vacuum tube revolutionized radio and gave birth to the electronic age.

But do you suppose the world quickly beat a path to the inventor's doorstep? It did not. So De Forest looked for some dramatic way to show what the tube could do. Enrico Caruso, the famous tenor, was to sing at the Metropolitan Opera House. De Forest set up his gear in a room above the Met and transmitted the sublime music to distinguished guests gathered about distant receivers.

The demonstration was a disaster. Spark operators, "rag-chewing" on the same wavelength, refused to give it up. All that the invited big shots could hear was a raucous jumble of dots and dashes.

Newspapers poked fun at the fiasco. De Forest's own backers decided he was a common swindler. He was hauled into court, charged with stock fraud, his "audion tube" pronounced worthless.

Barely escaping prison, the man who was in fact revolutionizing the Twentieth Century was sternly admonished by the judge to give up inventing and get a "common garden variety of job and stick to it."

(KCBS)

Early broadcasting experiments were carried out before World War 1 by **Charles "Doc" Herrold** (at right, in doorway) in San Jose, Calif. Note wind-up Victrola and telephone type microphone. The weekly broadcasts usually ended when Herrold's microphone burned up, due to its use to modulate the high voltage directly.

Herrold obtained 600 volts from nearby trolley wires, using long bamboo poles to hook on with.

Station **8MK** of the Detroit News makes its initial broadcast on August 20, 1920. The station (now **WWJ**) was the world's first to air programs on a daily, scheduled basis.

(The Detroit News)

A. J. Drummond
50 Fulton Street- New York
2/20/25   A
View of Wireless Room
S.S. Robert E. Lee

Many early broadcast engineers got their start in radio as shipboard wireless operators, or "brass pounders," serving weeks or months at a time at sea in wireless rooms like this one.

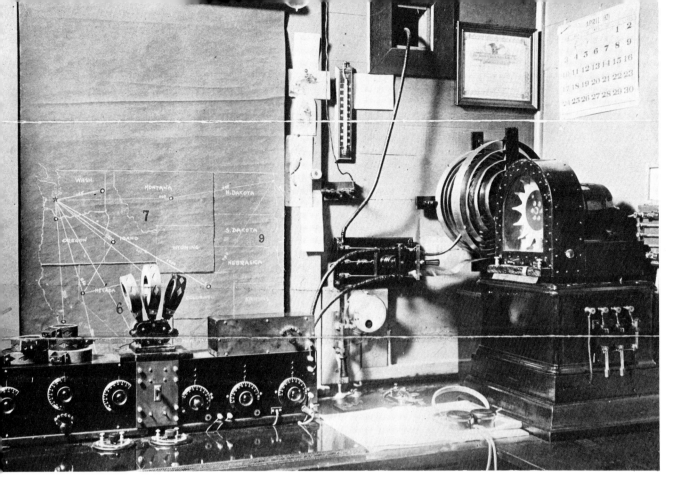

7YS, an early wireless telegraph station operated by Father Sebastian Ruth at St. Martin's College, Lacey, Wash. The map locates stations with which 7YS exchanged Morse code messages.

And now the crowning irony. Faced with a crushing debt of legal and other bills, De Forest was obliged to sell his patents. For just a few thousand dollars. Before long, they would be worth millions.

But De Forest didn't take Hizzoner's advice. He kept on inventing. In World War One, he helped the U.S. Navy equip its ships with wireless. After the war, he built an experimental station and for a time broadcast phonograph records. (A government inspector made him stop. "There is no room in the ether for entertainment," he said.)

But this was in 1919, and there was no stopping radio now. In Pittsburgh, Dr. Frank Conrad, assistant chief engineer for the Westinghouse Company, had an experimental station in the garage of his home. He too was playing phonograph records, to the delight of neighborhood enthusiasts listening in on home-made receivers. The following year he relicensed his station as 8XK and a kind of radio craze began sweeping Pittsburgh.

A department store began selling sets to people who didn't want to make their own. Conrad made a deal with a record store to keep him supplied, in return for mentioning the store on the air—history's first commercial!

8XK was taken over by Westinghouse late in 1920, and under its new call letters—KDKA—is generally recognized as the world's first broadcasting station.

Father Ruth's original "wireless shack" (radio building) on the campus of St. Martin's in 1914.

Seattle's first broadcaster, **Vincent I. Kraft**, in 1919.

But Frank Conrad was not the only amateur broadcasting from a garage in those days.

Out in Seattle there were dozens of radio buffs, many of them Army or Navy-trained in wireless, taking to the air with their own sets. The "hams" had theoretically been relegated to wavelengths below 200 meters. (Hence the term, "short wave.") Most were content to exchange messages in Morse code, using old-fashioned spark gear. But one slim, strong-minded youngster named Vincent I. Kraft had set his sights a good deal higher than that. Kraft reputedly built up the first set in the area to use a vacuum tube, and he began experimenting with sound transmissions.

Kraft's station was located in the garage behind his small hillside home at 6838 - 19th Northeast, not far from Ravenna Park. Tapestries were hung around the walls to help deaden the sound. In this makeshift studio were a microphone, a phonograph, a piano, and Kraft's little five-watt one-tube transmitter.

There was no fixed schedule of programs, but a handful of Seattleites who had crystal sets began listening in on his evening and weekend tests. Kraft would play records for them, or to vary the offering, invite a neighbor boy over to play the violin.

He continued operating in this casual manner for a couple of years, until the federal government acted to require special licenses and call letters for stations that were serious about "broadcasting" music and entertainment.

Kraft, who had been using the experimental call 7XC, decided to take the plunge. He applied for one of the new class of licenses, and on March 14, 1922, was informed of his new call sign. It was to be KJR. Broadcasting had arrived on Puget Sound.

(Tacoma Public Library)
A typical crystal set from the early 1920s. These sets required no electric or battery power. Radio energy collected by an outdoor long-wire antenna was converted to sound energy by touching the sensitive "cat's whisker" wire to a small chunk of galena crystal (shown here above the tuning knob). Sound was of quite good quality, but so weak you needed earphones to hear it.

Vincent Kraft (left, at raised table) was a radio instructor for the Seattle Y.M.C.A. Wireless School. He's shown here teaching a Morse code class about 1919.

Kraft was also experimenting with radiotelephone transmissions from the garage of his home at 6838 19th N.E. His station **7XC** (later **KJR**) was to be the Puget Sound country's first broadcasting station.

CHAPTER THREE

Aunt Vivian

Early one Monday morning back in April, 1912, a young American Marconi Company operator had sat drowsily at his post in New York, copying down the routine wireless "traffic" buzzing through his headset. Partly for business communications and partly as a publicity gimmick, the station had been located on top of John Wanamaker's department store.

Suddenly, a most un-routine message crackling through space caused the operator to sit bolt upright, rubbing his eyes in disbelief. "The S. S. Titanic ran into iceberg. Sinking fast."

For the next 72 hours, the young man with the soulful eyes and unruly hair stayed at his key, the nation's tenuous link with a great drama playing itself out in the icy Atlantic. Thus did the country learn of the disaster, the rescue efforts, the survivors and the victims.*

And thus did this young operator become a national celebrity.

The man was David Sarnoff. One day he would be the biggest mogul of American broadcasting. In fact, he came close to *inventing* broadcasting. In 1916, when he had become a Marconi Company executive, he was proposing to:

". . . bring music into the home by wireless. . . . The receiver can be designed in the form of a simple 'Radio Music Box' . . . supplied with amplifying tubes and a loudspeaking telephone, all of which can be . . . placed on a table in the parlor or living room, the switch set accordingly and the transmitted music received."

Besides music, he foresaw lectures and sports scores being transmitted via the "Radio Music Box."

Sarnoff's superiors didn't buy his idea. But by 1921 he had left Marconi to join a new outfit, and on April 29 of that year he was made general manager of the Radio Corporation of America. Then he lost no time looking for a way to get RCA into the fledgling business that would come to be called "broadcasting."

At that time a six-foot-one Coloradan named William Harrison "Jack" Dempsey was heavyweight champion of the world. Pro football hadn't been invented, so the national hysteria over blood sports was focused on the forthcoming title bout with France's champion, Georges Carpentier. The match was to be held at Boyle's Thirty Acres in Jersey City, across the river from New York. Sarnoff decided to broadcast the event.

RCA had no transmitter of its own, but the General Electric Company had just finished building one for the U.S. Navy and a young Undersecretary of the Navy named Franklin Delano Roosevelt said they could use that. Engineers installed it in a galvanized iron Pullman porters' shack at the Hoboken railway terminal.

Out in Seattle, news executives at the Post-Intelligencer decided to follow Sarnoff's example. Hastily they located a small transmitter and arranged for its installation on top of the P-I building at Sixth and Pine. It was tested and ready for business on Friday, July 1, the day before the fight.

Early next morning the crowds gathered. In those increasing numbers of homes where there were receiving sets. At stores around the city, where radios with loudspeakers had been installed on the sidewalks. On top of the Navy Yard Hotel, clear over in Bremerton. On the streets in front of the P-I. In the wireless shacks of ships, hundreds of miles out at sea.

According to the newspaper's own estimate, one hundred thousand people listened in as Dempsey proceeded to KO his opponent, in the fourth round, in an arena nearly 2500 miles away.

What all those listeners heard was not a blow-by-blow account. There were no remote originations yet, no networks, no sportscasters. At ringside, reporters dictated a brief summary of each round's action, and telegraphers relayed their descriptions on the nation's newswires. At the P-I, these bulletins were simply read over the air as they came in. Phonograph records from the Hopper-Kelly Company filled the time in between.

---

* Marconi had been booked on the *Titanic* but cancelled out before it sailed.

Seventeen-year-old **David Sarnoff** at a lonely Nantucket Island wireless station in 1908. Sarnoff had taught himself Morse code while working as a Postal Telegraph messenger in New York. In 1912, he would gain fame as the first operator in America to receive word of the *Titanic* disaster.

One of the first to see the possibilities of wireless as a broadcasting medium, Sarnoff rose to head RCA and later founded NBC.

Nevertheless, the Dempsey-Carpentier fight broadcast was a sensation. Everyone was talking about it. All around the Puget Sound country, radio fever was breaking out like some great, joyous epidemic. Parts stores could hardly keep receiving sets, crystals and cat's whiskers in stock.

So the P-I decided to make news broadcasts a regular part of its operation. They built a primitive studio in a shack on top of their building, accessible by an iron ladder leading to a trap door in the roof. To deaden the sound, they purchased canvas from Sunde & d'Evers, the ship chandlers, and draped it tent-fashion inside the shack.

A five-watt transmitter and other paraphernalia were installed by a local radio store. The paper announced that nightly news summaries would be read by a "man selected for the clarity and distinctiveness of his tones."

The man, who thus qualifies as the area's first professional announcer, was Carl Haymond. A former Navy wireless operator, Haymond was also the station's manager and engineer.

An inaugural broadcast of the station, KFC, took place on September 5. It included a baritone solo by Seattleite Bob Nichols, making the debut of his long and distinguished radio career. Carl Haymond discovered another part of his duties was to help guests like Nichols—no small man—to squeeze up the ladder and through the trap door.*

The next few months saw a spate of new signals taking to the airwaves. Longtime wireless experimenter Father Sebastian Ruth built a little five-watter at St. Martin's College near Olympia. Vincent Kraft put a station in St. James Cathedral for a short time. James D. Ross, president of Seattle City Light, personally supervised construction of a transmitter for the First Presbyterian Church.

* Babe Ruth and Texas Guinan were among those who climbed the iron stairway before this station's closing broadcast in September, 1924.

27

This log cabin on a hilltop at St. Martin's College, near Olympia, was built in the fall of 1923 and served as the studio for **KGY**, Father Sebastian Ruth's pioneer broadcast station. KGY (formerly **7YS**) had been relicensed for broadcasting the previous year. It was known on the air as "The log cabin station, where the cedars meet the sea."

Father Sebastian Ruth (second from right, in clerical collar) poses with a new piece of equipment outside **KGY**'s log cabin studio, about 1928. The salesman lays a proprietary hand on his "Permanent Radio Ground," a device claimed to solve all the problems early broadcasters were having with poor or "phantom" ground systems. The gadget did work wonders—but so would an old copper wash tub buried six feet down.

Seattle City Light Superintendent **James Delmage Ross** personally supervised construction of **KTW** for the First Presbyterian Church in 1922. This photo shows Ross (for whom Ross Dam is named) at work in the transmitter room, inside an ornamental dome high above the church roof. By this time (1925) partitions and a ceiling are in place. Earlier, the equipment was simply bolted to such beams and posts as passed through supporting the cupola.

KTW in the 1930s. The operator's "board" with announce mike and controls is in the rack at left. Patch panel connects with an attic studio (actually *below* the transmitter room) and church sanctuary, where the flamboyant Rev. Mark A. Matthews held forth with Sunday sermons.

29

KTW staff in the late 50's, after the station "went commercial"—broadcasting full-time and selling ads. Standing at left is station manager **Don Bevilacqua**, who has since had his own string of radio stations in Blaine, Bellingham and elsewhere. At the extreme right is announcer **John Sherman**, long associated with Christian and classical music radio in the area. Third from right, Chief Engineer **James S. Ross**, is a nephew of KTW's founder.

See Appendix for a discussion of KTW's claim to be "first in the Puget Sound Country."

The "**KGB** Radio Four" wowing them from the Tacoma Ledger's station in 1922. The musicians are **Roy Marzano**, "banjoist and leader"; **Roy Beckman**, saxophone; **Anna Luke**, pianist; and **Al Stewart**, drummer. **Al Stenso** (with headphones) is seated at the controls, with unidentified announcer at left.

The group's hit number was "Bow-Wow Blues," for which "chief announcer Alvin Stenso furnished the bark."

Note, at left, the musicians' microphone is an ordinary telephone to which a Victrola horn has been attached. Next to it is a telegraph sounder, complete with resonating tobacco can. All radio operators were obliged to listen for and relay distress messages from ships at sea in those days.   (Tacoma Public Library)

(Tacoma Public Library)

The July 29, 1922 wedding of Alvin Stenso and Miss Borghild Sivertson, broadcast live from **KGB** in Tacoma, was a radio sensation. Shown here are the **Rev. Ernest Bloomquist** (at left, and liable to trip over a microphone cord); **Frank Tovey**, assistant announcer, seated at transmitting panel; Tacoma Ledger radio writer **Al Ottenheimer** (the future actor) holding a megaphone-fitted carbon microphone; best man **John Hanson**; **Stenso**; **Miss Sivertson**; and **Esther Stenso**, the bridesmaid.

Howard Reichert, another radio buff whose experimental station 7XV later became KMO, was supposed to be best man at the wedding. For unexplained reasons he was replaced at the last minute by Hanson, who was Stenso's brother-in-law.

Meanwhile, in Tacoma, a flamboyant promoter named Alvin Stenso had assembled a station at the Tacoma Ledger's newspaper office.

Stenso was a charmer who had worked in a circus with "Buffalo Bill" Cody, survived torpedoing by a German U-boat, taught Morse code at the University. (Later he helped build the Tacoma Narrows Bridge— the one that collapsed.)

Stenso's station, KGB, was actually licensed the same day as the P-I's KFC; it apparently did not hit the airwaves, however, until early in 1922.

KGB only put out ten watts at first, and had an annoying hum. But Tacomans hailed it as the eighth wonder of the world. The programs were remarkable. Stenso, who was also KGB's manager and announcer, paraded everyone in Tacoma who could sing, play an instrument or make a speech before his microphone. Vaudeville acts playing the town were hardly off the train before Stenso had jollied them into the Ledger Building's burlap-draped studio.

And all for free, of course.

Stenso was a headline grabber, always coming up with something new. The station had been on the air only a few weeks when he announced he was getting

William Jennings Bryan, the Bible-quoting "great commoner," speaking over **KGB** during a trip to Tacoma. The aging orator and one-time Presidential candidate was one of the station's more illustrious visitors.

Bryan provided a dramatic moment during the 1924 Democratic Convention, the first to be broadcast by radio. Announcer Graham McNamee, transfixed, described the event over an early network of 18 eastern stations. When two delegates lost control in a debate and rushed at each other's throats, Bryan, praying loudly, threw himself to his knees between them to end the mayhem.

married—and that the whole ceremony would be broadcast over KGB, from wedding march to concluding kiss.

It was a radio first. A national news event. Police had to keep order among the fans crowding the newspaper building, hoping for a peek at the celebrated couple.

Another active enthusiast in 1922 was Louis Wasmer, whose main occupation was running the Excelsior Motorcycle and Bicycle Company store in Seattle. Wasmer came on the air in March with his own station, KHQ, and then built KDZE for the Rhodes Brothers Department Store at Second and Union Streets. He subsequently tired of Seattle, packed the apparatus for KHQ into the sidecar of his motorcycle, and moved to Spokane—where KHQ has flourished ever since.

It was Wasmer who built another of Seattle's earliest radio stations, KZC, at the Economy Market near First and Pike. KZC was a low-power station and had a very brief life, and like KHQ, its equipment was compact. When the station went off the air for good, its transmitter was pushed aside and forgotten. At some point workmen built a wall around it. But forty years later the wall was torn down, and there was this old transmitter with its strange hand-wound coils and unfamiliar tubes.

The FBI was called in—surely there were communist spies or saboteurs at work in Seattle!

But no, it was only a relic of early-day radio, and you can see it today at the Seattle Historical Society's Museum of History and Industry.

Motorcycle enthusiast **Louis Wasmer** established **KHQ** in Seattle in 1922. After a few years' operation there he packed the 100-watt station into a motorcycle sidecar and moved it to Spokane.

Pioneer broadcasting station **KHQ** after it was relocated in Spokane. Note the additions of a large bank of storage batteries along the right-hand wall, and telephone switching equipment on the table in the center of the room.

None of the early stations operated full-time, because there was only one wavelength authorized for broadcasting,* and it had to be shared. A typical day's fare for the Seattle listener began at 9:30 on weekday mornings, when KZC came on with tips to housewives about the day's best buys at the produce market. Then KDZE would take over with live or recorded music until 11, when KFC broadcast its first summary of the day's news. There were more newscasts at 2, 5:30, and 9:15 p.m.

KDZE, KJR, and KHQ alternated with entertainment programs during the remaining hours, except for certain periods when *all* the stations went silent. That's when radio buffs clamped their headphones on good and tight, and listened for the weak signals that might be coming from San Francisco, or Cleveland, or Peoria.

On Sundays, there was only one station on the air in Seattle. That was KTW, at the First Presbyterian Church. It broadcast religious programs all day.

On none of these stations would you hear a single commercial message. Broadcasting was strictly a public service—except for whatever glory accrued to the newspapers, stores or churches running the stations. In Washington, D.C. a Secretary of Commerce named Herbert Hoover summed up the general view:

It is inconceivable [Hoover said] that we should allow so great a possibility for service, for news, for entertainment, for education, and for vital commercial purposes to be drowned in advertising chatter.

Fair enough. What Hoover didn't say was how all that service, news, entertainment and education *should* be paid for. It was a question that would plague broadcasters for years.

Money was no big problem, though, when in 1924 Roy and Elise Olmstead decided to start a station of their own. True, the Olmsteads were a youngish couple, just married, and Roy had been dismissed from his job as a Seattle police lieutenant. But they were fairly rolling in money, and most of Seattle knew why. In those days of national Prohibition, Olmstead was undisputed "king" of the Northwest's largest ring of rumrunners and bootleggers.

Olmstead was no hoodlum, mind you. He never watered his whiskey, never threatened or hijacked anyone. He was a businessman and a gentleman, numbering his customers—and protectors—among Seattle's upperest crust. Nobody thought of big, square-faced, hearty and decent Roy Olmstead as a criminal.

He met London-born Elise Campbell in Vancouver, Canada. "Elsie," as Americans insisted on calling her, was vivacious and captivating. She spoke several languages, had studied music and traveled in Europe. It was her idea to start a radio station. Broadcasting, she was sure, was the coming thing. America's insane

* 360 meters—about 830 on today's radios.

Roy Olmstead, "king" of Puget Sound rum-runners. The former Seattle police lieutenant also owned and operated **KFQX**, one of the city's earliest radio stations, until federal "dry agents" closed him down.

experiment with Prohibition couldn't last forever, much as the Olmsteads would have liked it to.

So they bought a spacious old colonial house at 3757 Ridgeway Place in Seattle's Mount Baker district, moved in, and turned a spare bedroom at the rear of the second floor into a radio studio. Roy hired a bright young man named Al Hubbard to build the transmitter, which was to run a whopping 600 watts or more. It would be the Northwest's most powerful radio voice yet.

33

Hubbard had the rig built, tested and debugged by midsummer. Meanwhile he and Roy were getting on so well, Olmstead made him a lieutenant in his booze-running business. And so they went looking for another engineer. About that time an ex-railroad telegrapher namd Nick Foster blew into town, and he was hired to operate the new station.

Foster was another early experimenter in wireless telephony. In 1920, he and a one-armed sidekick, Jack Carpenter, had built an experimental station in Everett for the Kinney Brothers' music store. Carpenter subsequently left radio work to become—later on—superintendent of schools in Snohomish County, and Foster went to sea for the Alaska Steamship Company.

Now Nick was glad to have a shoreside job again. But it *was* disconcerting when just before he started, a

Nick Foster, Roy Olmstead's operator for radio station **KFQX**, in 1924.

Seattlite **Alfred M. Hubbard** was something of a mechanical genius with numerous inventions to his credit. He was the original operator of **KFQX**, Roy Olmstead's station, in 1924.

Hubbard became increasingly involved in rum-running activities on Puget Sound. His later claim to have been an undercover agent for Prohibition forces is open to debate.

government radio inspector gave him a blunt warning. "Watch your step with Roy Olmstead!" he said, cryptically.

Actually it was Elsie who ran the station. She thought up the programs, handled the finances, often appeared as the talent. To her the station—its call letters were KFQX—was a serious business, something quite distinct from her husband's more venturesome pursuits.

KFQX went on the air for four hours each night, beginning at 6:30 with stock market, weather, and news reports. This was followed at 7:15 by the station's most popular program of all: "Aunt Vivian" and her bedtime stories for children.

"Vivian" was Elsie herself. Legend has it that her sprightly yarns contained cleverly worded code signals to Olmstead's booze boats, waiting to land their secret cargoes at some unguarded shore. Roy and Elsie always denied it. Nick Foster was sure they had better ways than that to signal their boats.

But legends die hard, and throughout the Northwest today, this one still has its true believers.

"Aunt Vivian" (**Elise Olmstead**) broadcasting one of her famous bedtime stories for children. Legend maintains the tales actually were code messages for her husband's far-flung network of rum-runners.

Hear them on your Radio; (K-F-Q-X-)

(238 Meters—1000 Watts)

Dance with them at the Butler Hotel Cafe

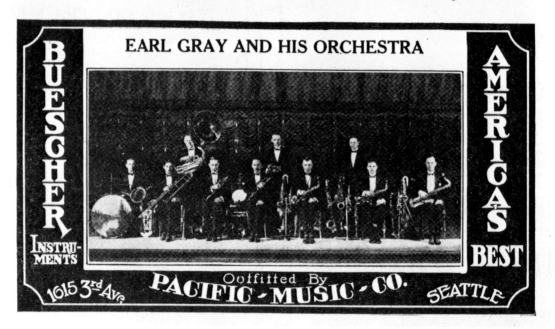

Ad for one of radio's first dance remotes. This was a new idea when the Olmsteads put one of Seattle's hottest bands on the air in 1924.

Plush **KFQX** radio studio in the Smith Tower, Seattle. Few broadcasts originated from here, though, as the station was raided by Prohibition agents soon after it was completed. Note the heavy sound-deadening drapes which were deemed essential in those days of "hissy" carbon mikes.

"Aunt Vivian" was followed by another of Elsie's innovations. For the first time in Seattle, remote lines brought live dance music direct from one of the city's most popular night spots. The swank Butler Cafe, at Second and James, was the "in" place for college blades to bring their girls and their hip flasks, and fox trot to the syncopations of Earl Gray's bouncy orchestra. Gray's nightly dance broadcasts from the Butler were an immediate sensation.

By November, Elsie was smelling sweet success. She was excited about getting sponsors for some programs —at $80 an hour. She wanted to broadcast concerts, plays, lectures. So she opened a plush studio downtown, on the twenty-first floor of the Smith Tower. It had expensive, heavy plum purple drapes suspended tent-like from the ceiling, for sound deadening; a piano; and an impressive carbon granule microphone hung on springs in an ornate stand.

But meanwhile, federal prohibition agents were stepping up a determined campaign to "get" Roy Olmstead. After work, when Nick Foster took a late Beacon Hill streetcar home, like as not he found the feds waiting there for him, asking all sorts of questions.

It was a mighty uncomfortable thing: the "Prohi" goons had a bad reputation. Foster played dumb and must have convinced them of his innocence, for at length they cautioned him that the Olmstead home was about to be raided.

Nick passed the warning to Roy, who only laughed. "Forget it," he said. "They wouldn't have the guts."

Besides, there was nothing incriminating in the house. No liquor. Only tea. The Olmsteads were inveterate tea drinkers.

Bedroom transmitting room of Roy Olmstead's **KFQX**, at 3757 Ridgeway Place, Seattle, in 1924. At right is engineer **Nick Foster**.

Then one dark, rainy-sloppy Monday evening, it happened. Elsie was in the middle of a fairy tale on the "Aunt Vivian" show. Roy and Al Hubbard were sprawled across Roy's bed down the hall reading funny papers. Nick Foster was hunkered down before a transmitter panel, eyeing the blue flicker of a suspicious power supply tube.

Suddenly, Nick felt cold steel against the nape of his neck, and a voice said evenly: "Turn that thing off."

When Nick looked around, he was facing the round end of a .45 automatic with the hammer laid back. He reached for the switch and pulled.

Elsie heard the rig go down, turned and gulped. The man with the gun was dirty and needed a shave. He wore no uniform and showed no badge. His shoes were dripping mud on the expensive carpet.

Elsie and Nick were ordered downstairs, where they found Roy and Al Hubbard already in the custody of half a dozen armed men, some of them brandishing sawed off pump shotguns. Among them Nick recognized Roy Lyle, head of the Seattle agents, and his assistant, Bill Whitney, who were personally directing the raid.

A search of the house turned up nothing more incriminating than tea leaves, but Lyle and Whitney were not to be denied. Going to the telephone and imitating Roy's voice, Whitney called up each of the Olmstead lieutenants, told them a party was in progress, and asked them to hustle over with a bottle of this, a case of that.

Whitney's wife arrived about this time. Having obviously practiced "doing" Elsie's voice, she placed some more calls. Soon the dining room was heaped with booze, the living room full of crestfallen bootleggers under arrest.

Around 4 a.m. the Prohi men herded their captives into waiting cars and started downtown in the rain. In one car was Earl Gray, the bandleader, who had innocently shown up at the Olmsteads' in the midst of the raid. All he wanted was to ask how the broadcast had sounded—not knowing he'd done the whole show into a dead mike.

MRS. OLMSTED CALLS COPS AS DRY AGENTS RAID HOME

WEATHER
Unsettled, probably rain tonight and Wednesday; not much change in temperature.
Temperature Last 24 Hours
Maximum, 55. Minimum, 41.
Today noon, 50.

The Newspaper With the Biggest Circulation in Washington

The Seattle Star

Entered as Second Class Matter May 7, 1899, at the Postoffice at Seattle, Wash., under the Act of Congress March 3, 1879. Per Year, by Mail, $5.00

Home Edition

VOL. 26. NO. 227. SEATTLE, WASH., TUESDAY, NOVEMBER 18, 1924. TWO CENTS IN SEATTLE.

Roy, His Wife and Guests Are Taken to Jail!

Released After Bail in Sum of $10,500 Is Posted; Federal Officers Say Alleged Liquor Ring Broken

DRY agents Monday night staged their long-promised raid on the home of Roy Olmsted, who has been called the "king of the bootleggers." As they broke in to the Olmsted residence at 3757 Ridgeway place, Mrs. Elsie Olmsted, hostess at a lively party, rushed to the telephone, according to W. M. Whitney, assistant prohibition director.

"Give me MA in-7810," she called. Then, hand over the receiver, she turned to Whitney, according to his story.

"I'll have this house full of police in a few minutes," she cried in defiance. "The police are with us."

An agent, at a sign from Whitney, roughly took the instrument from her and hung up.

While Mrs. William Whitney, aide to her husband, stood by and smiled, Whitney announced for the benefit of Mrs. Olmsted and the guests that: "This is my party. No one will come here that I don't want."

Olmsted, Mrs. Olmsted and 16 other prisoners captured at the Olmsted home were arraigned Tuesday before United States Commissioner H. S. Elliott, who, on November 12, issued the search warrant under which Whitney made the raid. The entire party, which had been held at the immigration station, was released. The Olmsteds arranged for and posted bail totaling $10,500. All pleaded not guilty.

Among the guests and prisoners was Mark B. Fleming, who describes himself as a home decorator, but who has been described by witnesses before city investigating committees as "a collector" for the police department. Fleming was prominently mentioned in the recent suspension of two city detectives and was accused of offering to have one of them reinstated upon payment of a certain sum. The charge never was proved and Fleming denied it flatly.

RAID FOLLOWED LONG EFFORT

Imported "under cover" agents of the prohibition department were given credit Tuesday by Roy Lyle, department head, for the success of the raid. They got the evidence and managed teh affair following several months of unproductive labor by the Seattle office, of which Lyle is the head and Whitney the assistant.

These imported agents have watched the Olmstead home for weeks. Twice they were on the verge of raid-making. Once, they said, they were prevented because a police prowler car came prowling thru the exclusive Mount Baker district in which Olmsted purchased his mansion.

When the raid was made Monday evening there was no resistance. The agents paraded before the guests with drawn revolvers, warning those in the house to make no outcry.

Others arrested include Ruth Bennett, Tom Takagawa, Japanese servant; Ed Engdohl, Phil Karanski, Richard Elbrow, alias Dick Bennett, Eddie Sadick, Louis Kleimen, Herb Fletcher, William J. Symonds, Clarence G. Healy, Carl E. Wilson, Hobart Hector, Isador Fischler and Myer Rose.

Clarence H. ("Baldy") Healy, said by Lyle to be one of the ring, was arrested later at his home, 625 E Lynn st., on a similar charge.

The arrest, according to Lyle, was made only after a carefully prepared case against Olmsted and his companions had been made. Warrants were issued by United States Commissioner H. S. Elliott November 17.

The complaints charge "the possession and sale of liquor on July 4, July 19, October 12 and November 17."

"Under cover" agents, unknown to the residents, have been watching the house for days. The name and address of every person who has visited the house in the past fortnight has been obtained by the agents.

According to Whitney, the meeting of the party was held "to direct the operations of Seattle's rum ring."

SEVERAL IN HOME ARE NOT HELD

Several persons who were present in the house at the time of the raid were not held, Whitney said. Included in these were Earl Gray of the Butler hotel theater orchestra; A. M. Hubbard, young inventor and operator of Olmsted's radio station, KFQX; Mrs. H. Fletcher and a man named Gearing.

Earl Gray declared he was at the home arranging for the remote radio control lines from the house to the Butler hotel.

Jerry Finch, Olmsted's attorney, was ready to post bail for all of the defendants Tuesday morning. Blank bail bond forms, issued by the National Surety Co., were ready for the insertion of the names.

The raid was conducted by Whitney, aided by Federal Agents Earl Corwin and James Johnson. Sam Ragsdale, private investigator for Prosecutor Malcolm Douglas, participated. Several under cover men, whose names are unknown, were stationed at various entrances to the building.

The agents entered the house first at about 10 o'clock, Whitney said. Two or three arrivals came afterwards and walked into the trap.

OVER-ZEAL ROBS THEM OF VICTIM

Sid Greene, said by Whitney to be

(Turn to Page 7, Column 4)

Olmsted's Mt. Baker Home and Principals in Raid

Neighbors of Roy Olmsted in the exclusive Mount Baker district heaved a sigh of relief today when they learned Roy Olmsted, his wife and a party of guests had been arrested by federal dry agents. The neighbors didn't like the idea of an alleged rum king living in one of the best houses of the district. Picture shows the beautiful home. Insets: Left, Prohiibtion Director Roy C. Lyle; right, Roy Olmsted as he appeared when he was a police lieutenant. Bottom, Assistant Prohibition Director W. M. Whitney.

Aunt Vivien's Bedtime Tales Rudely Checked!

Mrs. Olmsted Hoped Radio Would Win Husband Respectable Place in Society

BY JACK HALL

"Aunt Vivien," whose clear musical voice has told bedtime stories to hundreds of children radio fans over station KFQX, was in the U. S. immigration station Tuesday, facing federal liquor charges along with her husband, Roy Olmsted, and 16 others.

Few know Mrs. Olmsted. She is a London girl, a student, a musician and a vivacious, entertaining person. She has traveled extensively, studying her music in Italy. Somewhere, somehow, she met Roy Olmsted, declared to be the king of the Northwest liquor runners.

Since their marriage Olmsted has been reported to have been more or less retiring from his former occupation. He opened the 1,000-watt KFQX radio station and financed Alfred Hubbard, Seattle boy, who is working on several electrical inventions.

* * *

MRS. OLMSTED plunged into the radio work. She toiled long and hard to make the station the outstanding one of the Northwest. Some say she liked the work, for in it she saw the stepping stones on which her husband might make his way back into the respect of the community in which he lived.

She faced the obstacles that arose when it first became known that Olmsted was interested in the station. She laughed aside the criticisms and kept on at her work. She designed a broadcasting room like the rooms used by the singers in Italy for their practice.

Altho patient in her efforts to bring the station and her husband into the limelight of respectability, Mrs. Olmsted at times would flash fire at criticisms of Olmsted.

* * *

UNTIL Monday night "Aunt Vivien, the teller of bedtime stories, the moving spirit behind radio KFQX, the wife of Roy Olmsted, seemed to be making slow, painful headway. The station fans were increasing and the programs were coming easier.

Monday night her work of months was undone when the federal prohibition agents swept down on the Olmsted home and gathered her in with the rest.

And if "Aunt Vivien's" voice pierces the ether again with the stories of "Li'l Bre'r Rabbit" and of "Jackie Dumpling," it will be a new voice, perhaps softened, or perhaps hardened by the experience of a night and a day in the toils of the law, her first such experience in her new life.

Mrs. Harding Now a Little Stronger

MARION, O., Nov. 18.—Mrs. Warren G. Harding has survived another serious heart attack and now seems to be a little stronger, Dr. Carl W. Sawyer's 9 a. m. bulletin said today.

Red Lantern to Mark Dry Agents' Coup

A RED-GLOBED lantern with a yellow frame will hang from the top of the Thompson building, federal prohibition headquarters, tonight.

Some months ago agents of Olmsted, according to Director Roy C. Lyle, placed the lantern in the rear seat of a federal agent's automobile, as a joke.

"Keep that lantern here in the office," Lyle commanded his men. "It won't go out of here until Olmsted and his gang have been placed under arrest."

Tuesday, with Olmstead and 16 others under arrest on charges of violating the federal prohibition laws, the lantern was dusted off, filled with oil and made ready to hang from the flagpole on the top of the building.

Star Camera Man Mauled by Olmsted

ROBERT BRADLEY, a Star camera man, suffered at the hands of Roy Olmsted and his gang Tuesday noon. Bradley says he was hit in the jaw by Olmsted and was a jiu-jitsu victim of one of the Japanese in the Olmsted party, when he tried to take a picture of Mrs. Olmsted.

Olmsted and 15 others arrested in the raid Monday night were leaving the prohibition commissioner's office opposite the Lippy building on Third ave., after posting bail.

Bradley ran after Mrs. Olmsted and snapped a picture of her. Olmsted ran after Bradley, and the Olmsted party closed in on the camera man.

After throwing Bradley to the pavement, Olmsted, according to Bradley, smashed the expensive Graflex camera Bradley used, destroying the plates containing Mrs. Olmsted's picture.

When Bradley, dazed, picked himself up from the pavement, the party was a block down the street.

Bradly says that 100 spectators saw the fray, but made no move to help him.

Goodyear Co. Sued for Three Million

BROOKLYN, N. Y., Nok 18.—Suit for $3,000,000,000 for alleged breach of contract has been filed against the Goodyear Cotton & Rubber company of Akron, Ohio, it was learned today when attorneys for the company moved in supreme court to set aside service and complaint on the ground the service was defective. Plaintiff concerns are Stockton & Co., Morris & Co., the Taunton Manufacturing company and Thistle Cotton Mills.

Mrs. Olmsted Says She Was Slapped by Whitney

Wife of Alleged Rum Runner Describes Scenes That Followed Raid

"I WAS right in the middle of a bedtime story when the agents broke into the house."

It was Mrs. Roy Olmsted talking. She had just been released with her husband from the United States immigration station, where they were placed early Tuesday morning, following their arrest at their home on federal liquor charges.

"I was broadcasting over the radio and was stopped right in the middle of it. The men came in with search warrants which declared that they had knowledge there was liquor in the house.

"There were only half a dozen of us there. I let them look thru the entire place and they found nothing. When they couldn't find anything I expected they would leave.

"Bill Whitney refused to go so I called the police. He slapped me in the face, pushed me away from the phone and said I would call nobody."

"A man who knows me and knows I can talk several languages got suspicious and started to talk to her in German.

Mrs. Whitney said: 'Cut that stuff out and bring out the booze.' The fellow knew it wasn't me because I often talk to him in German. He didn't come out and they didn't have good luck after that."

"Then Whitney and the rest of the fellows began to call up bootleggers. They would say, 'This is Roy Olmsted. Bring out some liquor. We're having a party.'

"When the men would come out they would make them come inside and wait, and then would call more numbers.

"The agents would probably have had every bootlegger in town out there, only Mrs. Whitney, who was helping her husband, made a mistake.

"I'm not worried in the least," Olmsted declared. "The agents didn't find a drop of liquor in the house. Every bit they seized they got by calling up bootleggers' numbers. It wasn't my liquor.

"I've known Lyle was watching me for some time. It didn't bother me. There was nothing about my home that I was ashamed of or was afraid to let him see. Of course, I can't be responsible for the liquor Lyle brings in.

"We're going right back to broadcasting. The agents stopped us last night, a thing they had no right to do. They also arrested Hubbard, the operator, and are still holding him in the immigration station without a charge."

WIFE IS DEAD IN FURNACE

Pastor Is Questioned by Prosecutor in Death Mystery; He Finds Body

COLUMBUS, O., Nov. 18.—Insisting that he is as much baffled by the mystery of his wife's death as are the police, Rev. C. V. Sheatsley, pastor of the Lutheran church in the fashionable Bexley residential section, was dismissed temporarily today after a severe grilling by Prosecutor John R. King.

The pastor went immediately to the mortuary, where his wife's charred remains, which he discovered in the parsonage furnace, were being prepared for burial.

DEATH SHOCKS RESIDENTS

The death of Mrs. Sheatsley shocked the exclusive residential district of Bexley, where her husband is pastor of its leading church.

Coroner Murphy wanted to issue a verdict of suicide, but the prosecutor insisted that the whole thing be made the subject of a thoro investigation.

At the police station Rev. Sheatsley told the same story he had told the coroner. He arrived home last night after calling on members of his flock and found his older son, Milton, a student at Capital university, where Rev. Sheatsley has a Bible class, investigating the odor of burning flesh.

The boy said he had looked in the furnace several times before his

(Turn to Page 7, Column 4)

WOMAN IS DEAD IN CAR CRASH

Another Hurt; Two Men Held in Seattle Jail

One woman is dead, another injured and two men held in jail, after an auto crash near Auburn Monday night.

The dead woman is Mrs. Josefino Bastunaro, 29, of 510 Twelfth ave. S. Mrs. Louisa Traversa, of 1017 20th ave. S., is in Aubrn hospital with internal injuries. Adolph Jacconina, restaurant man, of Seattle, and Andy Sennimore, of Everett, who were in the wrecked car, are under arrest.

Police say that broken liquor bottles were found in the automobile.

The crash occurred on the highway near the Motor Inn. The Jacconina car skidded from the road, it is said, while traveling at high speed.

Each of the women has two minor children. Mrs. Traversa is the mother of Eva, 14, and Josephine, 12. The dead woman leaves Marino, 9, and Margaret, 11.

Home Brew

Howdy, folks! When a Seattle man is ordered to take a change of climate, all he has to do is to wait another day.

* * *

Federal judge in Maryland has ruled that a maker of home brew can't be pinched. Oh, Maryland! My Maryland!

* * *

The glove it is a startling thing—
Exciting, anyway;
It doesn't exactly scare you,
But it takes your breath away!

* * *

All the world's a stage, and a lot of us husbands have only thinking parts.

* * *

ABIGAIL APPLESAUCE SAYS:

"There's many a man who comes home late at night and tries to make noise like the wind blowing up the stairs."

* * *

Men with college degrees are now out of luck. Any old radio station can get just as flossy an array of letters behind its name.

* * *

Jackie Coogan says that he wants to be an automobile mechanic when he grows up. Isn't that just like Jackie? Always after the big money.

* * *

THE CROSS-WORD FAN'S OMAR KHAYYAM

A dictionary underneath the bough, a book of synonyms also, and Thou beside me in the wilderness searching for another word for "thou"!

* * *

This is National Education Week. Father will celebrate by sending his son at college another check.

* * *

I'd like to be
This Everett True.
He does the things
I'd like to do.

* * *

Rudolph Valentine, according to press dispatches, is growing bald. We always did tell Ruddy he shouldn't use so much Thousand Island dressing on his hair.

* * *

RUDDY HOME

Rudolph Valentino has returned home from a lengthy tour abroad with a mustache and beard that he grew while in Europe. He is pictured here as he was with his new alfalfa, which he intends shortly to train on a trellis.

* * *

Despite the fact that this is National Education Week, Li'l Gee Gee thinks that the three R's signify Rah! Rah! Rah!

* * *

Fame is a fleeting and ephemeral thing. What has become of the lads who wrote, "Yes, We Have No Bananas"?

* * *

Pupils in San Diego schools, according to Mayor Brown, are being taught that there is skating on Elliott Bay. Too bad there is no truth in the rumor. West Seattle residents, instead of having to cross the Spokane st. bridge, could skate home.

* * *

CANDIDATE FOR THE POISON IVY CLUB

The gink whao invented the key for sardine cans.

* * *

In the old days, Bobby used to ask his father to help him with his arithmetic. Now father asks Bobby to help him with his cross-word puzzle.

* * *

STRANGE, STRANGE GAL
IS HELEN STAIRS;
SHE DOESN'T YANK
OUT NEW GRAY HAIRS!

* * *

Song of the Scofflaw: "Be it ever so humble, there's no place like a Canadian liquor store."

* * *

YE DIARY

(November 17)

...ly up, and to reading "The Little ...ch Girl," which do be a book much ...up these days, but Lord! its action ...e spread over a vast number of ..., albeit it be interesting enough. ...me to the office, and there did some ... business, and then abroad, and to ... a record for my musick box, "Hard hearted Hannah, the Vamp of Savannah," and also some gum-drops for my wyfe, because when she do be ... of them, she can talk not at all. ...me to home.

* * *

"Mamma, mamma!" cried the young moth as it hovered over a pair of silk socks. "I've made a hole in ..."

* * *

... it please!

Don't You Dare Laugh at This!

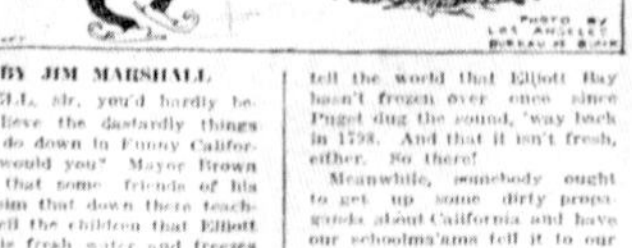

BY JIM MARSHALL

WELL, sir, you'd hardly believe the dastardly things they do down in Funny California, would you? Mayor Brown says that some friends of his tell him that down there teachers tell the children that Elliott Bay is fresh water and freezes over every winter.

"It's no laughing matter," says the mayor.

Why, of course it's not. We'd like to catch anybody laughing at it! It looks to us like another trick of the council efficiency committee to blacken the city's name, and we wouldn't be surprised if Ralph Nichols was mixed up in its somewhere.

Doc wants to send a delegate back to Washington and have the rivers and harbors congress tell the world that Elliott Bay hasn't frozen over once since Puget dug the sound, 'way back in 1798. And that it isn't fresh, either. So there!

Meanwhile, somebody ought to get up some dirty propaganda about California and have our schoolma'ams tell it to our children. We have faked up a sort of catechism on the subject, for use in elementary, or grade schools.

Comme ca:

* * *

WHO is the American consul in Los Angeles?

Who runs the blacksmith shop in San Francisco now?

What was the name of the Iowa professor who heard Los Angeles was a seaport and spent 27 years walking around trying to find the ocean?

Who first thought up the joke about there being only two kinds of weather in California—perfect and unusual?

How many ships were sunk in the last tidal wave in San Francisco bay?

Describe the seven kinds of animals found in Los Angeles drinking water.

Who first thought of affixing to a small and obscure knoll in Northern California the title of "Mount Shasta"?

Name the seven slum districts in San Diego.

Who was the press agent who first thought of describing California earthquakes as fires?

Rewrite the story of Californian who, after arrival in hades, wired back to Bakersfield for his blankets.

* * *

THAT'S just a rough outline of the plan. With a little working over, it ought to be possible to convince the kiddies, as they are sometimes referred to, that California is bounded on the north by the hoof-and-mouth disease; on the west by heavy fog, on the south by moving picture persons and on the east by the poignant moans of disillusioned Middle Westerners.

"Hic Jacet California," says Mayor Brown, making a rotten Latin pun.

Well, hic jacet Puget sound right back at 'em.

Nick Foster was in another car with Roy and an Olmstead deliveryman known as "the gardener," a man famous all over Seattle for his tattered clothing and body odors. Bill Whitney was driving, his wife sitting on her knees next to him, facing backwards and laughing hysterically as she waved a cocked .45 at her frightened prisoners' noses.

At the federal lockup, Earl Gray and Nick Foster were turned loose. The Olmsteads and Al Hubbard were later released on bail.

The liquor ring was smashed. Federal prosecutors, using wiretap evidence, built a celebrated case against Roy and Elsie that would keep their lawyers busy for years—a case that would go all the way to the Supreme Court.

Meanwhile, a trusted Olmstead bookkeeper stuffed most of the liquor empire's cash into the pockets of a trick overcoat, pointed his souped-up Stutz Bearcat toward Canada and was never seen again.

Suddenly, money was very important to the Olmsteads after all.

Nick Hight Foster (right) about 1964, instructing student broadcast engineers at Edison Technical School in Seattle. The school operated **KCTS** Channel 9 for twelve years.

Nick Foster started as a railroad telegrapher in 1916, went to sea as an Alaska Steamship Co. "sparks" and was operator of Roy Olmstead's radio station during its brief career. A lifelong advocate of vocational education, Foster taught electronics in the public schools from 1926 to 1940, and at Edison (now Seattle Community College) until his retirement in 1971.

CHAPTER FOUR

"Blend's Mah Friend"

Oliver Williams Fisher, born in a backwoods Ohio log cabin, never reached the fourth grade of school. His people were too poor. But by the time he passed fifty, "O. W." with his five sons had built an empire of lumber and flouring mills and stores, stretching from Louisiana to Montana.

In 1906 O. W.'s third son, Oliver David Fisher, was in Montana reading in a paper about the great earthquake and fire that had just leveled San Francisco. He got to thinking. All those homes and businesses would have to be rebuilt. It meant a tremendous market for West Coast lumber.

So "O. D." switched his headquarters to Puget Sound, and started cruising for timber. And in another twenty years, the Fisher family interests in the Northwest would grow to include not just timber and flour milling, but banking, insurance, real estate and—broadcasting.

Here's how it happened.

Early in 1925 the Olmsteads leased KFQX to a young advertising man named Birt Fisher. Now this stocky six-footer with the cheerful blue eyes was unrelated to the flouring mill family. He had been a lineman with his father's telephone company around Spokane. Later, he had a little signboard business in Seattle, along with a nickelodeon concession on the Black Ball ferries running out of Coleman Dock.

Fisher changed the station's call to KTCL. (There was a vogue at the time to use call letters that "stood for" something, and the Puget Sound country was being widely promoted as "The Charmed Land.")

He moved the station's transmitter to 3215 - 29th Avenue West, on top of Magnolia Bluff, set up a studio in the New Washington Hotel basement, and began broadcasting from there early in April.

Fisher hired an engineer, a salesman, and a secretary. The announcing he did himself, in a deep, commanding voice. Programs ranged from live dance music by Warren Anderson's orchestra to a series of educational broadcasts for Seattle high schools.

But KTCL was always in a financial bind, due to Fisher's lack of capital. The station was licensed for 1,000 watts' output power now, but this required four hundred-dollar transmitting tubes, and Fisher never could afford more than two of these at one time. Whenever he saved enough for two new tubes, two old ones burned out, and he was right back where he started.

And it was getting harder and harder to meet the station's bills. Early in 1926, KTCL was evicted from the New Washington and had to remain silent until Fisher arranged for new quarters in the Home Savings Building, at 1520 Westlake.

It was about that time that Roy Olmstead's liquor conspiracy trial ended in his conviction. The former "king of the rumrunners" was fined $8,000 and sentenced to four years at hard labor. So Olmstead, needing cash, sold his stock in KTCL to Vincent Kraft. Kraft announced big plans for the station, once the Fisher lease expired.

But Fisher had been bitten deep by the broadcasting bug, and he didn't intend leaving the field so easily. After all, all he needed was some money! So he went looking for an angel. His first stop was the Harbor Island office of Fisher Flouring Mills, Inc. Perhaps he thought the coincidence of the last names would get him past the front office, at least, and so it did.

By an even happier chance, Oliver David Fisher turned out to be a radio fan of the first water. In fact the fruit cellar of his Laurelhurst home just bulged with storage batteries powering the various receivers in an upstairs room, where O. D. spent his evenings listening for far-off signals. The idea of starting up a local station, and making it one of the nation's best, seemed too good to pass up.

And O. D.'s brother Will Fisher, who ran the flouring mill, figured the station would promote sales of Fisher's Blend flour.

So the Fisher family made Birt an offer. They would put up two thirds of the capital to form a new company, to be known as Fisher's Blend Station, Inc.

Birt would put in the other third and manage the station.

Birt moistened his lips and confessed he had no money.

Well, said the Fishers, we'll loan it to you.

Fisher's lease was due to expire in a matter of weeks, so orders were rushed off for the new equipment, including a fine modern transmitter; and all of it would be of first-class manufacture—no "home brew" gear at all.

A three-story concrete building was hastily poured on Harbor Island, back of the flour mill, to house the one-kilowatt rig. Two lofty pairs of telephone poles—the tallest they could find—were strapped together

Officers of FISHER'S BLEND *station Inc.*

O.W. FISHER
President

DAN R. FISHER *Vice Pres. Treas.*

BIRT F. FISHER *Secy-Manager*

The men who founded **KOMO** in late 1926. **Orin Wallace Fisher** and **Dan R. Fisher** were members of the powerful Fisher family empire of lumber, banking and flour milling interests on Puget Sound. **Birt Fisher** (no relation) secured their backing to refurbish the station he leased from rum-running king Roy Olmstead, after Prohibition agents put it off the air.

Fisher's Blend delivery trucks were a common sight on Seattle streets in the early 20's. The influential Fisher company was to establish the region's top radio station, **KOMO**, and later **KOMO-TV**, tieing "Fisher's Blend Station, Inc." closely to their flouring mill ads.

Warren Anderson's orchestra broadcast daily over **KTCL** and its successor, **KOMO**. Anderson (standing, left, with drum sticks) had a jazzy style and drove his band hard, playing by the hour with hardly a pause for breath. (That was before the day of long-winded commercials.)

Charles Lindbergh broadcasting over **KOMO** on September 13, 1927, shortly after his historic solo flight from New York to Paris. Lindbergh landed at Sand Point and made several appearances in Seattle, including this one at the University of Washington stadium.

and raised perilously into the sky with the station's antenna. (For years, on picking up any telephone at the mill, you could hear the radio station playing softly in the background.)

A deal was made with the Metropolitan Building Company, another Fisher concern, to trade studio space in the Cobb Building basement for advertising.

Meanwhile, Birt Fisher had applied for a new call sign. KTCL had been repeatedly linked to bootleggers in newspaper reports of the Olmstead trial, and he felt a change was called for. He asked for the letters KOMO, not that they stand for anything—he just liked their sound. That change took place in August. What's more, Fisher got government approval to transfer the call to his *new* station when it came on the air at year's end.

Fisher's lease of the old Olmstead station didn't end until a few days into 1927, so for a short time he would be operating two stations at once: the old KOMO, that is, the former KFQX-KTCL, which now became KGFA*; and the big new station.

The new KOMO's inaugural broadcast began at 3 p.m. on the last day of December, 1926. It was unlike anything Seattle had known before. By the end of New Year's Day, some 250 people had taken part, including the station's full-time house orchestra. And everything

was live. It would be years, in fact, before KOMO condescended to broadcast even one recording.

By now separate wavelengths had been assigned each radio station by the government, and Fisher was able to plan a solid fourteen hours of broadcasting every day. He had fairly scoured the Northwest for talent, signing up all the best singers, instrumentalists, actors and announcers. KOMO became the largest employer of musicians in the state.

Everything was to be first class, and the accent was very much on culture. Over half the programming in the station's first year would be serious music.

To bankroll this amazing operation, O. D. Fisher had gone to the Seattle business community and signed twelve of the largest concerns into a unique corporation known as Totem Broadcasters. In effect, each participating business pledged to underwrite its share of all unsold broadcast time. In return there were brief on-air acknowledgments of each firm's sponsorship.

These were not the full-blown commercials of today, and the advertisers had no say at all in when their ads would be read. Ken Fisher, who was a KOMO announcer in 1927, recalls that their messages were simply used on a rotating basis, one every ten minutes or so.

* After Vincent Kraft took the station back he changed the call yet again to KXA.

(Seattle Historical Society)

KOMO's **Mark** "Iron Mike" **Wienand** (right, with headphones) broadcasts primary election returns from Seattle P-I's editorial room, Sept. 11, 1928. It was the first time listeners could get details of an important election as fast as they came in, and all against a bedlam of genuine newsroom sounds: clicking telegraph sounders and typewriters, reporters' phone calls and cries for "Copy boy!" and even Prudence Penny's staff of home economists offering coffee and snacks.

One announcement, which Fisher still remembers, went like this:

"The orchestra will now play von Suppé's 'The Light Cavalry Overture' (or whatever) in the interests of Wild Rose Lard, produced by Charles H. Frye and Frye Packing Company, the largest packing company in the world."

The Fisher Flouring Mills Company was itself part of Totem Broadcasters. Its messages plumped Fisher's Blend Flour with the slogan "Blend's Mah Friend," quoting the smiling black chef whose picture graced this product's package.

Station breaks identified KOMO as "Fisher's Blend Station" and Will Fisher had guessed right: flour sales were never better.

There were five other full-time radio stations in Seattle just then—1927—but Ken Fisher recalls that KOMO's only real competition was with the Rhodes Department Store station, now relicensed as KFOA.

Not that KFOA had anything like the Fisher company's facilities, program talent or financial resources.

KFOA's studio had been on the second floor of the store, where shoppers were invited to pause and "observe the work of broadcasting." Typical of early broadcast installations, there was a black upright piano, a table with several wicker chairs around it, a record player, carbon granule microphones, and lots of mysterious wires and equipment hanging about the walls. Now Rhodes had moved into newer quarters in their next-door Arcade Building's fourth floor. But they still played a good many records and filled time with "radio talks" of doubtful interest.

KFOA, though, had one thing which KOMO didn't: a new-fangled something called network affiliation. Just weeks before the Fisher station took to the air, KFOA had signed up with David Sarnoff's newly formed National Broadcasting Company.

NBC's grand inaugural broadcast took place on November 15, a mind-boggling four-and-a-half-hour national event. The hookup featured Walter Damrosch and the New York Symphony Orchestra, singer Mary Garden and humorist Will Rogers, with live originations from various parts of the United States.

And even as KOMO was presenting its own inaugural on New Year's Day, KFOA was luring listeners with a play-by-play broadcast of the Rose Bowl game down in sunny Pasadena, California. It was the first live coast-to-coast sports broadcast ever, with a colorful pioneer announcer-singer named Graham McNamee at the mike.*

Network radio was another of Sarnoff's early dreams come true. In 1922 he had envisioned it as a gigantic public service effort, rather like a library, to be supported by philanthropists, or maybe a cut from the profits of radio set sales.

Advertising would be barred, he thought.

But Sarnoff was stymied then because the American Telephone and Telegraph Company, which owned the nation's long-distance lines, refused to make them available. Instead, A. T. & T. proposed to start its own network. It began early in 1923 with a two-station linkup, and made history the following year, feeding a rather dry election eve speech by not-so-silent Cal Coolidge coast-to-coast to 22 stations, including KFOA in Seattle.

Then in 1926 A. T. & T. abruptly retired from the field, and NBC was hastily formed as a subsidiary of RCA, which was itself a combine of radio manufacturers headed by the General Electric Company. (Hence the notes G, E, C of NBC's "bong, BONG, *bongggg*" chimes.)

NBC was announced to the nation in full-page newspaper ads, with RCA's chairman calling it a "semiphilanthropic...investment in the youth of America." The investment was modest, though. In its first year there would be no daily schedule of programs. Just a few special events of national importance.

But more and more top shows were planned to come down the line later, and O. D. Fisher was determined to get KOMO plugged in. By February he was in New York, pushing and shoving, and finally he clinched the deal.

O. D. returned to Seattle with not just an affiliation in his pocket, but plans for organizing a separate, intramural hookup of NBC stations on the West Coast. This Pacific Coast Network (or "Orange net," as it came to be called) exchanged some 340 hours of entertainment and events programming between the major far Western cities during 1927. NBC's Eastern net fed specials like the World Series and Charles Lindberg's triumphal return from flying the Atlantic.

It wasn't long after this that KFOA switched its ownership, its call letters, and its affiliation. Reborn as KOL, this station signed up with NBC's newly organized rival, Columbia—then a shoestring subsidiary of the phonograph record company—and afterward with another West Coast web, named for its founder, a wealthy, balding Cadillac dealer named Don Lee.

* McNamee's great talent was making even dull games sound exciting. Once somebody asked NBC President Merlin Aylesworth how much McNamee actually knew about football: "Damned little," Aylesworth replied, "but he certainly puts on a great show."

Sydney Dixon (left) and **G. Donald Gray**, a popular vocal duo in the 1920s. Dixon's voice was a sweet tenor. Gray, a baritone, doubled as an announcer over **KOMO**. Having started out singing opera in Leeds, England, he had the broad stage-British voice considered the ultimate mark of culture and authority for announcers in those days.

Sally Jo Walker was a popular vocalist on **KJR** in the 20's. Note spring-suspended carbon granule microphone of the early type. These mikes would periodically go "dead" until someone jarred the granules loose, usually by rapping the mike against a table-top several times.

Studio "A" of **KJR**, home station of the **American Broadcasting Co.**, Seattle, 1929. Note announcer's desk with its mike, telephone, and control panel for turning microphones on and off. It seems wicker furniture also was *de rigeur* for high-class studios of the 20's.

There was another pioneer Seattle station changing hands about the same time. Vincent Kraft's KJR was sold to Adolph Linden, the businessman-banker who owned the Home Savings Building where KJR's studios were located. Linden started up an ambitious all-live operation on the top floors of the building, no doubt hoping to emulate KOMO's success.

Linden built up an impressive staff of lavishly paid announcers, singers and musicians, including a dance band, a symphony orchestra, and a marvelous string trio. Visiting performers of prominence often added to the inspiring bustle around KJR's studios. One might bump shoulders with Paul Whiteman, Marian Anderson, Meredith Willson or the great operatic tenor, Tito Schipa.

When Schipa first walked into KJR's Studio "A" he tested its deadened acoustics with some powerful "Ahhhs" and "MMMnnns," and shouted, "No! No! No! Impossible. I cannot sing in here!"

No use explaining the room's heavy drapes and rugs were necessary to compensate for the carbon microphones of that era, which otherwise tended to hiss. Finally a resourceful announcer found Schipa a

square of plywood to stand on, so he could feel the resonance, and he went on.

For much the same reason, announcers quickly got in the habit of cupping a hand behind one ear while at the mike, by way of monitoring their own voice quality.

Adolph Linden was a solidly built man, always well groomed. Soft-spoken. Liked by everyone. Some of the crew called him Daddy Linden, after the benevolently prosperous Daddy Warbucks in the comics.

Because Linden rarely came around the studios. He stayed in the background, paying the enormous bills that rolled in, and working toward his shining dream: to build a great national network with KJR as the key station. He called it the American Broadcasting Company.

Besides KJR, Linden owned KEX, Portland, and KGA, Spokane. Later he acquired KYA in San Francisco, and by the summer of 1929 had signed up sixteen more outlets, from Bellingham to Chicago. East Coast stations were due to come on the line later in the year.

"Just me and my radio." **Francesco Longo** was director of the American Philharmonic Orchestra, which played frequently over the **ABC** from Seattle. Here Longo poses with a battery-less console radio, the latest thing in listening, about 1929.

Hot stuff around 1929! This popular trio played the classics over **KJR** and Adolph Linden's ABC network.
From left: **Peter Merenblum**, **Cecile Barron**, and **Kolia Levienne**.

"Harper's Corners," a folksy dramatic series originating at **KJR**, drew more fan mail than any other feature on Adolph Linden's ill-fated American Broadcasting Co. After **ABC**'s debacle the show was resurrected as a three-times-a-week series on several Northwest stations, at one point using *two* live orchestras for background music and bridges.

Written by Mitchell Sutherland, the scripts starred **Burton James** as the barber, **John Pearson** as the constable, **Al Ottenheimer** as "Grandpa Prouty" (who claimed to have "fit in every battle of the Civil War") and **Robert Keef** as "Budge Talbot."

Publicity photo of the "Haywire Logging Co.," locale of a series of radio sketches by Seattle author Jim Stevens. The plays were carried over the **ABC** in 1929. They were suggested by Stevens' best-selling books which had elevated the Paul Bunyan of lumber camp myth into a national folk hero.

Stevens was promised $50 each for the plays but had to sue for his money when the ABC went bankrupt.

Linden's ambitions seemed boundless. Once ABC was firmly established as a top radio chain, he planned to go into movie-making as well. He had an option on property near his Lake Forest Park estate, and was already dickering with some Hollywood movie people about working for his operation. Meanwhile he had sponsored two summer series of lavish outdoor concerts in University Stadium, and was even negotiating for an airplane to attempt history's first non-stop flight between Tokyo and Seattle.

All these enterprises were costing huge sums of money. But then, Adolph Linden was also vice-president of a local savings and loan company, and somehow, the bills got paid.

But a judge decided the "somehow" was embezzlement, and Linden wound up behind bars.

The blow fell suddenly and without warning. Paychecks ceased abruptly, and most of the staff left. The telephone company yanked out connecting lines to the other stations. A local music store repossessed whole truckloads of grand pianos.

Thomas Freebairn-Smith, a young announcer still with the burr of his native Scotland to his voice, pleaded over the air for someone to donate a piano. Someone did—an ancient but playable upright. The station's receiver-in-bankruptcy advanced fifty dollars for phonograph records, since the station couldn't afford them, and a few faithful employees kept the station going.

When the dust of reorganization finally settled, another banker was in control. He was Ahira Pierce, head of another savings and loan.

Map shows extent of the ill-starred **American Broadcasting Co.** (no relation to today's ABC) which collapsed in 1929. Founder Adolph Linden was on the point of adding more stations when he was arrested for embezzling funds of the Puget Sound Savings & Loan Association.

"Tommy" Freebairn Smith, Scottish-born announcer on **KJR** and the short-lived **American Broadcasting Co.** After the network's demise in 1929, his pleas to listeners brought an old piano and phonograph records to keep the station going.

SOLONS FIND ALASKA'S NEED IS MORE ROADS

House Farm Committee Sees New Lake And Cows Crossed With Yak On Northern Trip

By E. B. FUSSELL

More roads are the big need of Alaska.

This was the view expressed by members of the house sub-committee on agricultural apporpriations, who returned to Seattle yesterday on the coast guard cutter Tahoe from a three-week tour of the territory.

MANY REQUESTS

"We had more requests for roads than for any other form of aid," said Representative John W. Summers of Washington, only Western member of the committee, who acted as guide for the party.

Alaskans, Summers said, are already talking hopefully of the day when a projected international highway, from Seattle to Fairbanks, can be constructed, allowing millions of automobile tourists to visit the world's best summer resort.

As an example of how little of Alaska's immense area has been explored thus far, members of the party related the discovery during their trip of a large lake, only a few dozen miles from Juneau. Its existence had not previously been suspected.

WILL AID INDUSTRY

Maj. R. Y. Stuart, chief forester of the United States, who accompanied the party, said last night the lake would be of immense importance in developing pulp projects in the vicinity of Juneau. It will provide approximately 25,000-horse-power.

Congressmen L. J. Dickinson of Iowa, chairman of the subcommittee; John N. Sandlin of Louisiana and James P. Buchanan of Texas were other members of the party. All the congressmen were accompanied by their wives. Miss Jean Summers, daughter of the Washington congressman, also was a member of the party.

Breeding experiments at the agricultural college at Fairbanks, in which hybrid cattle have been produced, interested the congressmen.

BRED WITH YAKS

By crossing Galloway cattle with yaks from the steppes of Thibet, a breed has been developed, intended to provide both milk and meat, and

---

TODAY'S BROADCAST

Air Time Table

MORNING

6:30-12—KRSC. Music, etc.
6:45-12—KOL. Music, studio programs, etc.
7-12—KFQW. Studio program and musical records.
7-12—KXA. Music, etc.
7:55-10:15—KOMO. Inspirational services, music, etc.
8-11—KPQ. Musical records.
8-12—KJR. Health exercises, music, etc.
10:15-10:30—KOMO. Prudence Penny's home hints.
10:30-12—KOMO. Music, etc.

AFTERNOON

12-12:30—KOL. Records.
12-6—KXA. Records, etc.
12-4—KPQ. Musical records.
12-12:45—KOMO. Music, etc.
12-5—KVL. Musical records, etc.
12-6—KJR. Varied music.
12-6—KFQW. Musical records, etc.
12:30-1:30—KOL. Kiwanis Club.
1-6—KOMO. Music, etc.
1:30-2:45—KOL. Music, etc.
2:45—KOL. Baseball game.
4-4:15—KPCB. Musical records.
4:30-6—KPCB. Records, etc.
4:30-6—KOL. Studio program.
5-5:30—KVL. Religious program.
5:30-6—KVL. records.

EVENING

6-8—KRSC. Music, etc.
6-10:30—KOMO. Music, etc.
6-11—KXA. Music, etc.
6-12—KJR. Music.
6-11:20—KPCB. Music, etc.
6-12—KOL. Music, etc.
6-12—KFQW. Records, etc.
10:30-10:45—KOMO. Late news and sports by Post-Intelligencer.
10:45-12:30—KOMO. Music, etc.
12-6 a. m.—KFQW. Records, etc.

KXA—526.6 m (570 kc)

7-8:45 a. m.—"Sunshine Jack."
8:45-9 a. m.—Watch Tower program.
9-10 a. m.—Uncle Ash-Madeline Lattier, piano; Chris Coughlin, tenor.
10-10:30 a. m.—Inspirational services; organ program.
10:30-12 noon—Sunshine hour, etc.
12-1 p. m.—Time signal and weather; Jimmie Golden, piano; organ recital.
1-2 p. m.—Popular recordings.
2-3 p. m.—Hawaiian program.
3-4 p. m.—Bridge party hour.
4-5 p. m.—Song and piano recital.
5-6 p. m.—Popular recordings.
6-7 p. m.—Goldie, piano; George Knight, tenor; Elvira Herman, kiddies entertainer.
7-8:30 p. m.—Studio program.
8:30-8:45 p. m.—Aloha Harmony Singers.
8:45-9 p. m.—Studio program.
9-10 p. m.—Concert.
10-11 p. m.—Bill Winder's Dance Orchestra.

KRSC—267.7 m (1120 kc)

6:30-9:45 a. m.—Stock reports; musical klock.
9:45-12 noon—Records, etc.

KOMO—325.9 m (920 kc)

7:55 a. m.—Inspirational services.
8 a. m.—NBC system; Happy Time.
9 a. m.—Concert orchestra and soloists; Madelin Dvorak and Dorothea Wei, solos and duets.
10:15 a. m.—Prudence Penny of Seattle Post-Intelligencer: "What to Prepare for Dinner."
10:30 a. m.—NBC system; women's magazine of the air.
11:30 a. m.—Recorded entertainment.
11:45 a. m.-12:45 p. m.—Popular Orchestra; grain reports; orchestra and soloists.
1 p. m.—Concert orchestra and soloists.
2 p. m.—NBC system; The Wanderers.
3 p. m.—Concert orchestra with G. Donald Gray, Helen Hoover and Greenwood Mitchell.
4 p. m.—Resume of evening's programs; stocks and bonds; children's stories; Madelin Dvorak and Dorothea Wei, duets; Dorothea Wei, contralto; Helen Hoover and Fred Lynch, duets; stock, bond and grain quotations.
5 p. m.—Popular Orchestra with Art Lindsay and Fred Lynch.
6 p. m.—NBC system; Eskimos (transcontinental).
6:30 p. m.—NBC system; Orchestradians (transcontinental).
7 p. m.—NBC system; Neapolitan Nights and Hello Murs (transcontinental).
8 p. m.—NBC system; Tales Never Told.
9 p. m.—NBC system; "The Family."
9:30 p. m.—Concert orchestra with vocal and instrumental soloists.
10:30 p. m.—News flashes furnished y Seattle Post-Intelligencer.
10:45 p. m.—Harry Krasnoff, piano.
11 p. m.—NBC system; musical Musketeers.
12 midnight—Theatre organ.

KJR—309.1 m (970 kc)

8-9 a. m.—Morning Serenaders.
9-9:30 a. m.—Better homes program.
9:30-9:45 a. m.—Novelty program.
9:45-10 a. m.—Devotional service.
10-11 a. m.—American Popular Orchestra.
11-12 noon—Olympic Rangers and Anthony Euwer, "Philosopher of the Crossroads."
12-12:30 p. m.—World in review; talk, "America Meets the Orient." Dr. H. H Gowen.
12:30-1:30 p. m.—American Artistic Ensemble; soloists, Perdin Korsmo, Hallie F. Strude.
1:30-3 p. m.—Talk, Dr. Stevenson Smith, "The Well Trained Child"; American Salon Orchestra; soloists, Sydney Dixon and Ve Ona Socoiofsky.
3-4 p. m.—Anderson's Orchestra.
4-5 p. m.—Damski's Neapolitans; soloists, Perdin Korsmo, Merle North.
5-6 p. m.—Paul Whiteman, "Hour From Hollywood."
6-7 p. m.—Collegienne; American Artistic Ensemble.
7-8 p. m.—Show Boat.
8-9 p. m.—Soloists, Perdin Korsmo, Merle North; "Histories of Paul Bunyan."
9-10 p. m.—American Philharmonic Orchestra; soloists, Agatha Turley and Nathan Stewart.
10-10:30 p. m.—Enchanters Male Quartet.
10:30-11 p. m.—Celeste Sextette; soloists, Loren Davidson, Merle North.
11-12 p. m.—Anderson's Orchestra.

KOL—236.1 m (1270 kc)

6:45 a. m.—Radio time clock.
7 a. m.—"Eye Opencer."
8 a. m.—Radio time clock.
9:45 a. m.—Studio program.
12 noon—Organ recital.
12:30 p. m.—Kiwanis Club luncheon.
2:45 p. m.—Baseball game.
4:45 p. m.—News, weather, etc.
5 p. m.—Studio program.
7 p. m.—"Old Uncle Henry," Frank Coombs.
8 p. m.—Hal Chase, finance talk.
9 p. m.—"A Little Sunshine," Ken Stuart.
9:30 p. m.—Margaret Gray, piano.
10 p. m.—Studio program.
10:30 p. m.—Kol Jamboree.

KFQW—211.1 m (1420kc)

8-8:15 a. m.—Request program.
8:15-9 a. m.—Early Birds.
9-11 a. m.—Popular records; home helps.
11-12 noon—Symphony hour.

'BING' CROSBY ON AIR TODAY

"Bing" Crosby of Spokane known in the popular song world for his eccentric singing style, wi entertain the nation tonight vi radio. He is slated as soloist wit Paul Whiteman's Orchestra for broadcast through CBS-ABC stations at 5 o'clock, Pacific time.

Crosby is programmed for thre numbers, "Satisfied," "Vagabon Lover" and "Good Little, Bad Li tle You." Tunful dance numbe listed for orchestral interpretatio are "Referrin' to Her 'n Me," "La Night Honey," "Waitin' at the En of the Road," "Sleepy Valley "Jericho," "Satisfied" and "Let Do It."

* * *

Alluring tango tunes of yesterd and seductive modern love balla will vie for popularity on KOMO 9:30 o'clock program this evenin going out over Northwest Triang stations. Charles Stay, barito will assist the concert orchestra Stay has selected such numbe as Bartlett's "A Dream," "Sylvi by Speaks, and Ball's "Ten Tho sand Years From Now."

* * *

Changing their time on the from Saturday to Tuesday, KOl Jamboree frolickers have a nine minute show for dialers tonig The whoopee partly starts at 10: o'clock featuring the Light Siste "Ban, Joe and Eddy" and the C ver Leaf Trio.

KVI—394.5 m (760 kc)

7-11 a. m.—Records.
11-12 noon—Organ concert, etc.
12-2 p. m.—News flashes; records.
2-3:15 p. m.—Loren Hollenbeck, ter Betty Harding, contralto; Leonard Cornick, piano; records.
3:15-4 p. m.—Songs. Betty Harding Loren Hollenbeck; Hawaiian music recor
4-6 p. m.—Records; Dorothy Grod soprano; Bob White, baritone; records.
6-7:30 p. m.—Flossie Steeves, sopra Leonard McCormick piano; Dance orchest Billy Landers, soloist; mixed quartet.
7:45-8:15 p. m.—Concert ensemble.
8:15-9 p. m.—Radio skit, Joyce Booth Maurice Penfold; concert trio.
9-10 p. m.—Dance orchestra with solo 10-11 p. m.—Concert ensemble; songs, White and Dorothy Grodvig.
11-12 midnight—Concert trio; organ cert.

Sleuth Charge Liquor 'Frameup

TACOMA, Aug. 19.—(Special Protesting his innocence and claring that liquor interests h "framed" him, W. W. Winga fifty-two, head of the Northwest tective Agency, who was arres in a raid on his offices Saturd night, still was in the county this evening in default of $1, bail.

Deputy Prosecutor Ray C. R

Radio listings for Seattle stations in August, 1929. Note the heavy schedule of live productions on **KJR**— which was just two days away from sudden bankruptcy. Some of KJR's shows were by arrangement with CBS, including an early appearance by Bing Crosby, then touring with Paul Whiteman's band. (In the accompanying article, the P-I felt obliged to explain who "Bing" Crosby was, putting the as-yet little known nickname in quotes.)

Vic Meyers poses with his Club Victor dance band in KJR's studio "B" around 1930.

Dapper Vic Meyers, leader of a popular dance band which was the rage of Puget Sound airwaves in the 20's and 30's. Meyers later turned to politics and served several terms as Washington State's lieutenant-governor.

"Hi" Pierce was a thin, emaciated little man, who reminded one of the diffident bookkeepers in Charles Dickens's novels. He hired a manager to run things, realistically rechristening Linden's little group of surviving stations the "Northwest Broadcasting System."

The staff remained small, with everyone filling two or three jobs at once. Still, Pierce claimed he had the largest payroll of any station in the Northwest, and KJR was once again producing all-live programming of good quality.

There were, for example, the highly popular broadcasts by the smooth Club Victor dance orchestra of dapper, mustachioed Vic Meyers. (Meyers later capitalized on his new-found fame, running for mayor of Seattle as a joke. He lost, but decided in the process that the real politicos were not a bit smarter than he after all. He filed for lieutenant-governor of the state for real—and won.)

Broadcasting frequencies were not jam-packed with signals as they are today, and distant ones were easier to pick up. There were no "Hooper ratings" yet, but there were other ways of knowing where the listeners

Here comes the Maxwell House "Show Boat!" Seattle-born **Lanny Ross** (second from right) was one of the stars of network radio's biggest variety show in the early 30's. Ross attended Madrona School as a boy and used to ride in bicycle races around Green Lake. He studied law at Yale but his sweet, clear tenor voice led him to the Juilliard School and a 1928 debut on radio.

From left: **Herbert Hohler**, **Frank McIntyre** as the "Captain," soprano **Winifred Cecil**, "Aunt Maria" (**Irene Hubbard**), **Irene Dunn**, **Ross**, and **Walter Castle**.

Oddly enough, for the first two years on "Show Boat" Lanny wasn't allowed to speak. Actor Allyn Joslyn read all his lines for him.

were. KJR and KOMO, for instance, had fans stretched from Alaska to the Pacific Islands, and well into the Midwest.

Sometimes, though, one wished there weren't so many people tuned in. Like the time KJR was presenting a dance program with Vic Meyers' orchestra. The musicians played their introductory bridge, and the announcer suavely named the next number. It was a popular ditty of that period, called "She Sits Among the Sheltering Palms."

Only he bobbled the second word.

There was no way to take it back, of course. Everything was live in those days. The band stopped— nobody could blow any more. One violin managed a few squeaks and the pianist tinkled in desperation. Meyers swung his baton furiously and at length, they all got through the song.

Then the telegrams started coming in. One was from Omaha, demanding to know who that anouncer was, "cr . . . ing all over the United States!"

And that's how KJR learned there were listeners in Nebraska.

Bob Nichols was one of those who left Seattle around this time for greener pastures in California. Speaking over NBC, he had a similar problem with a line for Eastman Kodak—something about shooting snapshots of ships at San Francisco.

He ran through all the possible mutations of this particular blooper, trying to get it right, and never did. Finally, announcers learned just to keep going when they made such mistakes. Nine times out of ten the listener would decide he hadn't really heard what he thought he heard, if he noticed the "fluff" at all.

KJR had lots of listeners, all right, but not enough sponsors. After running the station for two years, "Hi" Pierce was still losing money at an alarming rate. Incredibly, he fell into the same temptation as his predecessor, and wound up in prison for misappropriating funds of the savings and loan company, which went suddenly bankrupt one fine day.

And that was the end of the Northwest Broadcasting System.

Meanwhile, NBC was extending a second network to the Coast—the two chains were designated "red" and "blue"—and wanted another outlet in Seattle. So NBC brass were prevailed on to buy KJR as their Blue Network station on Puget Sound. They made numerous changes, but the station was still losing money a year later.

And NBC was itself in financial trouble. Late in 1929 the nation's overloaded economy had begun popping all its fuses, first in the frenzied counting houses of a famous New York thoroughfare, and finally in the lesser empires of Main Streets everywhere. David Sarnoff had just moved his huge operation into some enormously costly quarters, called Radio City, in New York's Rockefeller Center. What with the astronomical rents, and a lot of philanthropists jumping out of skyscraper windows at the time, Sarnoff was rethinking his ideas about the funding of network radio.

(Broadcast Pioneers Library)

Far and away the biggest thing on early radio was the mildly racist comedy of "Amos 'n' Andy," played by (white) actors **Charles Correll** and **Freeman Gosden**, a couple of one-time radio singers in Chicago. They are shown here in a burnt-cork publicity pose.

The series started in Chicago in 1926, gradually spread to the East Coast and reached Seattle in the fall of 1929 as a six-nights-a-week series.

Everything came to a halt when "Amos 'n' Andy" came on. Throughout America theaters, interrupting or delaying their movies, piped the show to audiences who would otherwise have stayed home. President Coolidge left word not to disturb him during the program. Telephone surveys showed over half the nation was tuned in—though many listeners wouldn't answer their phones while the show was on! Quipped the Seattle Star:

"A bunch of the boys were whooping it up in the Malemute Saloon,
The kid who twisted the radio dials had captured a jagtime tune;
When suddenly out of the ether there came a program they all deemed dandy,
And cards were dropped as sourdoughs stopped to listen to 'Amos 'n' Andy.'"

Another factor was the phenomenal success of NBC's competitor, the Columbia chain, now that a young cigar company heir named William S. Paley had become its president. Paley didn't know the first thing about radio at first, but he knew plenty about business, and he wasn't buying any nonsense about semiphilanthropic investments in the youth of America. What CBS wanted to do was make money, and CBS was doing it, year after year, in spite of the Depression. NBC hadn't shown a real profit yet.

Now that would have to change. NBC executives dropped their opposition to all but the most blatant ads, began actively courting advertising dollars, and looked for ways to cut losses.

When their collectively jaundiced eyes fell on KJR's sorry balance-sheet, they got in touch with KOMO's O. D. Fisher. There was a bit of corporate arm-twisting, and Fisher's Blend Station, Inc. found itself with not one but two radio stations to run.

KOMO and **KJR** shared this transmitter building and 570-foot antenna tower on Seattle's West Waterway after the Fisher company acquired the second station in 1933. The new installation is pictured here shortly after its completion in April, 1936.

CHAPTER FIVE

Pioneers and G-Men

It is a remarkable thing that despite the very real problems of the businessmen who were trying to stay solvent as broadcasters, radio *as an institution* actually soared to its best heights in the ill wind of Depression. Suddenly, Americans in their millions were tuning in. (What else was there for a nation—dismayed, idled and impoverished by such bewildering events—to do?)

By 1930, radios didn't need batteries any longer. The box-like receiving set, with its dimly lit dial and cathedral top, just plugged into the wall. Better circuits inside filtered away the worst squawks and whistles, and you didn't even need an outdoor antenna.

No way was radio a toy any more. Now it was music to lift sagging spirits. It was escape through the make-believe of drama. It was the reassurance of a Presidential chat.

And it was *free!*

Meanwhile, the broadcasters were making their marriage of convenience with advertising, which began pumping in more money—and so better programs—than the philanthropists ever did.

Thus did the Golden Age of Broadcasting dawn above the wreckage of Wall Street's "Black Tuesday."

America's newspapers, however, didn't take kindly to radio's rebirth as an important advertising medium. To make matters worse, broadcasters—alert to the great yearning of people everywhere to understand just what in blazes it was that was happening to them—were devoting more and more time on the air to news.

In the twenties, newscasts were brief, some stations lifting them verbatim from the columns of local papers. KOMO in its first year only averaged about twenty minutes of news a day. It was read by newspapermen into a microphone at the P-I Building.

KJR had an arrangement with the Times. When a major news event broke, the mighty whistle atop the Times' old triangular building at Fourth and Olive would shriek, while an assistant city editor named Hal Burdick hustled two blocks down the street to broadcast the story.

(Burdick later went to NBC and starred in his own dramatic show, with a newspaper office setting that could well have been patterned after the Times. It was called "Night Editor," and the multi-voiced Burdick played all the parts.)

By the early thirties, a serious rivalry had grown up between radio and the press. Some local papers refused to print program schedules any more, or if they did, gave only the briefest information. Sponsors' names were taboo. Thus, "The A & P Gypsies" appeared as just plain "Gypsies."

Now broadcasters had to supply their own news announcers and ticker service. But even the new agencies imposed conditions. News bulletins were limited to thirty words a story—hardly more than headlines—and had to end with the words: "For further details, consult your local newspaper."

When KOMO and KJR began their combined operation, it was decided the former station would concentrate on quality music and entertainment. KJR became the duo's special events outlet, and a young telephone company employe named Bob Ackerley was hired to do several newscasts a day.

Ackerley had a pleasant but business-like baritone voice with a distinctive bite to it. He was billed as the Totem News Reporter. Once, staff announcer John Heverly booted his introduction, proclaiming authoritatively: "Your TOOTEM NOSE reporter is ON THE AIR."

It was hard to do the news for days and days after that.

News broadcasts during **KOMO**'s first years were read by Post-Intelligencer reporters from a radio room in the P-I building. Clockwise from upper left: "Prudence Penny" (**Bernice Redington**) giving advice to homemakers; "Sunshine" (**Doc Wilson**) and "Sparky" (**Don Milligan**) solicit gifts for the P-I Christmas fund—note tuxedos sometimes worn by early announcers, even in audience-less radio studio; **Walter Rue**, P-I radio editor, reporting late headlines; **Willard Coghlin** reads the late evening news (in more comfortable shirtsleeves); and **Art Chamberlin** recaps the day's sports events.

In July 1933, the two Fisher's stations moved into new quarters occupying half of the seventh floor in the Skinner Building, on Fifth Avenue. There were four large, superbly equipped studios, along with announce booths, control rooms, sound effects storage, client's booth, offices, etc. The two largest studios had suspended spun-glass ceilings, three-foot walls, and floors mounted on balsam wool. And all put together with glue—there were no nails anywhere.

It was said to be the finest broadcast facility west of Chicago.

The operation was novel, too. Programs from any studio could be fed to either station. Announcers, musicians, writers and equipment were all shared. With KOMO on the Red net and KJR on the Blue, control buttons for the two stations were colored to match. A single announcer at station break time could push one and say "This is KJR," push the other one and announce "This is KOMO."

Sometimes, of course, somebody would get mixed up and announce the wrong station. A then teenager named Howard Duff, scarcely out of Roosevelt High School when he joined the staff, is the supposed record holder for getting mixed up most often. Duff later carved out a career as radio's "Sam Spade" and went on, as they say, to movie stardom.

58

(Seattle Historical Society)

Studio "B," one of four deluxe studios built for **KOMO-KJR**'s combined operation on the seventh floor of the Skinner Building in Seattle, July, 1933. The construction was something marvelous. Floors floated on six inches of balsam wool. Walls, doors and ceilings were double; and glue, rather than nails, held things together. It was one of the finest broadcast installations in the world.

(Seattle Times)

"When you hear the roar of the presses...the newsboy's voice...the sound of the newsroom... it's time for NIGHT EDITOR, featuring **Hal Burdick**!"

Burdick, one-time law student at the Unversity of Washington, was an assistant city editor at the Seattle Times during radio's formative years. Part of his job was reading news flashes over **KJR**. A talented writer, actor and raconteur, Burdick wound up with NBC, starring in his own show. As "night editor" of a great city newspaper, he would recount tight, well-plotted stories in which he played all the parts himself.

Ted Bell, a big, likeable bear of a man who'd played football at Broadway High and the University of Washington, broke into radio on Mary's show. He earned fifty cents a program for reading poetry. Another regular, Grant Merrill, was piano accompanist for whatever singers Mary "happened" to spy strolling along the paths of her mythical garden.

Merrill was a dashing Richard Halliburton type. He had taught English in Turkey, hobnobbed with the queen of Rumania and once spent a night perched atop an Egyptian pyramid. He was continuity director at KJR, and had an entertaining program of his own, discussing the use and derivation of words.

Almost everybody doubled in brass in those days.

One of Seattle's top shows as the thirties began was the "Mardi Gras Hour," another variety program heard mornings on KJR. It starred (among others) a tall young singer, Elmore Vincent, billed as the "Texas Troubadour."

Actually, Vincent grew up on a loganberry farm in Oregon. The farm went broke and Elmore, still a teenager, went to work in a Tacoma sawmill. He learned to sing with the help of phonograph records and piano-playing girl friends, and began pestering

Elmore Vincent (left) and **Grant Merrill**, stars of **KJR** and the short-lived Seattle-based American Broadcasting Co.

Elmore Vincent as "Senator Fishface." Vincent was a young singer on **KJR** in the 20's. He invented the Fishface character as a joke but it led to a lifelong career on network radio and early TV.

Until the thirties, live radio generally meant music, lectures, poetry readings, hog prices. A popular show in Seattle was "Mary's Friendly Garden," which combined everything but the hog prices.

"Mary" was Velva Weller, a phenomenally voluble and enthusiastic young woman whose sheer torrents of high-flown poetic verbiage boggled the mind—and ears.

Mary was one performer who never used a script. Never at a loss for words, she occasionally wished she'd chosen different ones. Like the time she was commenting on the glamor queens of Hollywood, and suggested in all seriousness they "wouldn't *be* so glamorous if you took away their clothes!"

Live music on **KJR** when it became Seattle's NBC Blue Network outlet in the early 30's. From left: **Casey Jones**, **Abe Brashen** (with violin), **Elmore Vincent**, **Sally Jo Walker**, **Marshall Sohl**, and **Al Schuss**.

every radio station within hitchhiking distance for a job.

Finally, when KJR got into its financial bind, he was hired at the whopping salary of $32.50 a week to sing on seven or eight programs a day, six to seven days a week. There were other duties too—like setting up microphones between programs, and running the duplicating machine.

As a lark, one morning on "Mardi Gras" Vincent unveiled a comedy character of his invention, "Senator Fishface." Fishface, who later acquired the given name Frankenstein, was a lovably outrageous bumbler whose Freudian slips parodied all second-rate politicians everywhere.

"My fellow chiselers—er, citizens," Fishface might begin a garbled campaign speech. "My record reeks—er, speaks for itself!" Then he would promise everything from free feedbags for sea horses to featherbeds for the town jails—"to attract a better class of prisoners!"

Beginning in 1932, NBC picked up "Mardi Gras" for its Pacific Coast net, and soon afterward Vincent was lured away to the big time. He parlayed the Fishface shtick into a long career on the networks, first in radio comedy and then as one of television's pioneer dramatic performers. You've probably seen him most recently as the toothy grandpa on McDonald's commercials.

61

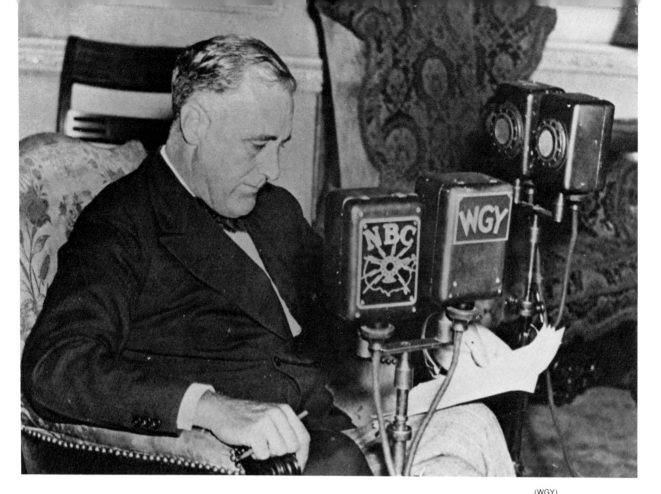

Franklin Delano Roosevelt was the first American politician to speak intimately, through radio, with a vast audience. His "fireside chats" from the White House would become famous; but Roosevelt used the technique even before he ran for President. Here, as governor of New York, he speaks to the people of that state over **WGY**.

By 1930, broadcasters were mastering a new literary form known as radio drama. In earlier years, some stations had tried broadcasting ordinary stage plays by hiding microphones in the footlights. But the results were not good. Radio plays needed to be specially written for the mind's inner eye, using sounds alone.

NBC pioneered the new genre with a series called "The First Nighter." The success of these half hour plays from "the little theater off Times Square"—actually the program came from Chicago—ushered in an era of dramatic programs ranging from soap operas and whodunnits to movie adaptations and science fiction.

(The acknowledged high point of realistic radio fantasy was to be Orson Welles' "War of the Worlds" broadcast which would frighten listeners half to death in 1938. The extraordinarily vivid sound pictures of Welles' Martian invasion convinced thousands the story was true, despite frequent disclaimers that it wasn't.)

A good deal of radio drama was produced by Puget Sound stations. Perhaps the best-remembered series of all was called simply "Pioneers." It was written by Hector Chevigny and sponsored by People's Bank.

Each episode dramatized an exciting historical event, such as the time in 1908 when two Seattle cable cars slipped their grips and went careering down the Yesler Way and James Street hills. For that one, sound men built a long inclined trough on which cannon balls were rolled to get the right effects of the runaway cars.

"Pioneers" aired on Sunday nights and was directed by John Pearson, an announcer-singer at KOMO-KJR. The actors were largely recruited from theater groups around Seattle and from the University of Washington's drama department. Bit players (Pearson called them "Indians") earned fifty cents a broadcast, enough for carfare and lunch, with a whole nickel left over.

"Chiefs" who took leading roles got as high as three dollars.

Fred Patterson, director of Seattle's Cornish School, played in many episodes. Howard Duff took roles occasionally, while studying drama at the "U." Al Ottenheimer was a regular, also starring as "Mr. Wyde-Awake" in an early quiz show.* Later he was on Broadway in "West Side Story."

---

* The show drew big crowds to downtown theaters and paid as high as $100—a lot of money in the late thirties—for right answers, based on current news items. The show was sponsored by a local tea and coffee company. As a gimmick they would station a costumed tea leaves reader in the theater lobby.

Producer-director **John Pearson** was responsible for many fine dramatic programs on the radio in the Pacific Northwest, including "Pioneers," written by Hec Chevigny. Pearson started out in vaudeville at 16, graduated to serious drama and appeared in movies before coming to Seattle.

Albert Ottenheimer was producer-director of "So Goes the World" and emcee of the "Mr. Wyde-Awake" quiz show. A fine actor, Ottenheimer appeared in many early radio plays and later was on Broadway in "West Side Story."

(University of Washington)
Frances Farmer and **Don McQuade** rehearsing for the **KJR** drama "Empire Builders" in 1934.

Farmer later became a nationally famous film and radio star. McQuade stayed in Seattle and was a prominent actor, announcer and sound effects man.

Burton W. James produced many of Seattle's earliest radio dramas. James came to the Northwest via Boston and New York theaters to teach drama at the University of Washington. He and Mrs. James were active for many years at the Cornish School and the Seattle Repertory Theatre as well.

Dave Harris was a frequent actor in "Pioneers," "Seattle Streets," "Across Horizons," and other dramatic offerings. Harris also played Santa Claus for the Frederick & Nelson store for many years. His son, Stanley, following in Dave's footsteps, was a KOMO announcer for a while. Then he went to Chicago and played the part of "Jack Armstrong, the All-American Boy" nationwide for Wheaties.

Another regular on "Pioneers" was a strikingly beautiful co-ed named Frances Farmer. Frances started at the "U" in journalism, switched to drama and was clearly headed for stardom. She was extremely poor, sometimes showing up for a radio part barefoot, with a piece of rope for a belt. Later she starred in movies with Cary Grant, Bing Crosby, John Garfield and many other Hollywood greats, besides appearing on Broadway and in major radio shows.

Tragically, Frances was a loner who always felt unloved. She spent several years in the State hospital at Steilacoom, a victim of depression and alcohol, and died of cancer in 1970 even while staging a comeback as a movie hostess on TV.

Hec Chevigny, who wrote the "Pioneers" scripts,

was a slim, radiant youngster from Montana, who'd wanted to be a doctor. In 1928 he took a job at KOMO, writing continuity and advertising copy, to finance med school. Then he discovered he had a flair for writing, and decided to stick with it. Later he went to Los Angeles, wrote a movie, books and magazine articles, and radio scripts by the hundreds.

His radio credits include action series like "Mr. and Mrs. North" and the soap operas "Portia Faces Life" and "The Second Mrs. Burton."

Chevigny went blind suddenly while still quite young. But he overcame his handicap, resumed writing, and achieved considerable fame with a tender book about life with a seeing-eye dog. It's called *My Eyes Have a Cold Nose.*

"Pioneers" began on KOMO, later switching to KOL, where dramatic background music was added by organists like Don Isham and Ivan Ditmars. KOL's studios in the basement of the Northern Life Tower, as the Seattle Tower was known then, housed a mammoth studio organ, one of the largest of its kind anywhere. Daily organ concerts were a regular part of KOL's schedule for many years.

Hector Chevigny, one of radio's most respected writers, began his career in Seattle with the program "Pioneers." It dramatized early events of Puget Sound history. Chevigny later lost his sight, but continued to turn out top-flight scripts for radio's "theater of the mind."

Photo at right (courtesy Gonzaga University) shows Hector Chevigny and "Wizard." Besides radio scripts and articles, and several books on Alaska, Chevigny wrote a tender best-seller about his life with a Seeing Eye dog.

Actor **Dave Harris** had a long career spanning radio's best years. A versatile man, Harris also played a department store's Santa Claus to generations of Seattle youngsters.

Wendell Niles went from leading a small dance band in Seattle to announcing some of the nation's most prestigious shows: Bob Hope, Burns and Allen, Milton Berle—the list goes on and on. In the days of live TV drama, he was the voice of both "Climax" and "Shower of Stars" on CBS.

Tacoma-born **Art Gilmore** started in radio as a singer on his own show over **KVI** in 1934. He worked as an announcer on **KOL** before moving South to Hollywood where he acted on shows like "Lux Radio Theater" and, when TV came along, "Dragnet" and "Adam-12." He was Red Skelton's announcer for 16 years.

Gilmore is a past president of AFTRA (the broadcast artists' union) and founding president of the Pacific Pioneer Broadcasters' Association. Today, he's the announcer on "Sears Radio Theater" and "I Believe in Miracles," and is narrator for the "Layman's Hour" and "Drivers Digest."

Busy **Ivan Ditmars**, talented pianist and organist, hails from Olympia. He was studio manager and Ken Stuart's accompanist, among other jobs, at **KJR** in the early 30's. Later he moved to **KOL**, where he often entertained at the station's mighty pipe organ in the Northern Life Tower basement. Ditmars eventually went to Hollywood and a career playing organ backgrounds on many outstanding radio and TV shows.

Trevor Evans studied drama at the University of Washington in the early 30's, acting in such theaters as the original Penthouse (atop what is now the University Tower Hotel). Graduating at the depth of the Depression he played in stock companies and was a freelance radio actor before joining **KOMO** as a writer. He wrote and acted in many radio productions during his 42-year career as Seattle broadcaster and adman.

Another KOL show in the mid-thirties was "Junior G-Men," a kids' adventure series sponsored by Ener-G cereal. The kind of show where for a box-top and ten cents you got a badge, password and secret code.

The thrice-weekly program starred Howard Duff as the "Chief" who broke all the cases. There was an uncanny resemblance to the "Sam Spade" character he would make famous a few years later.

Wendell Niles, a former Seattle band leader, was the program's original announcer. Niles left Seattle after a bit, to seek his fortune in Los Angeles and New York. He found it, too, as announcer for such greats as Bob Hope and "Lum and Abner." His brother Ken also hit the big time, announcing top network shows like "Abbott and Costello," "Beulah," and "The Danny Kaye Show."

(Ted Bell recalled there was an inside joke in the thirties. If you got fired at KOL, well, you took a train south and were sure to make it big in L. A.)

After Wendell Niles, a lanky Tacoman named Art Gilmore announced the "G-Men" show for a time and then *he* went to CBS in Los Angeles. He announced the "Dr. Christian" program, among others, and later appeared often on TV. He can still be seen as Captain Didion, the watch captain, in reruns of Jack Webb's "Dragnet."

"Junior G-Men" was written by Trevor Evans, a stock company actor just out of college. He also played many parts on the "Pioneers" series and wrote continuity for KOMO-KJR.

"G-Men" had a low budget, and the scripts didn't pay much. After he took the job, Evans found he was also expected to ditto the scripts, do the sound effects, and if the script called for more than three people, play all the excess roles himself!

But Evans was good at changing voices, and especially gifted at dialects. He wrote himself into the show sometimes just for the sheer great fun of it.

Oh, radio was fun. Every screwy, lovely minute. Ask anybody lucky enough to have been part of it. Their eyes will gleam as they tell about the marvelous, marvelous times.

Nobody got very rich, mind you.

But they all loved it.

"All I want is the facts, Captain!" **Art Gilmore** appears with **Jack Webb** on "Dragnet" from TV's early days. Gilmore (right) played Webb's boss, "Captain Didion" of the Los Angeles Police Dept.

CHAPTER SIX

"The Friendly Station"

By the later thirties, radio had hit its stride with top-flight dramatic programs like "Lux Radio Theater"; comedy shows with Bob Hope, Fred Allen, Jack Benny and others; action thrillers such as "The Shadow," "Gang Busters," and "The Lone Ranger."

There was nothing like today's live coverage of breaking news, though, and recordings were still largely *verboten*. So important world events had to be recreated by actors. This was done, nationally, on a phenomenally popular weekly network program, "The March of Time."

Seattle had its own version, called "So Goes the World." It aired on KJR each Sunday night, and had an impressive following too. One of the show's writers was Tacoma-born Tom Griffith, then a Seattle Times staffer who later became senior editor of Time Magazine.

Griffith remembers the show's cast as competent actors who could produce numerous voices and accents as required. But the one essential voice which made the whole program convincing was that of President Franklin Roosevelt. It was Howard Edelson's impeccable re-creation of FDR's familiar delivery that really put the show across. Edelson also "did" Hitler, Mussolini, and other prominent personages of that time.

"I think we used only FDR's actual words," Griffith recalls now, whereas "The March of Time" was once denounced by Stephen Early, the White House press secretary, for putting words into FDR's mouth.

"In memory, we overdramatized the news, inflating crises breathlessly. But on reflection, it is hard to exaggerate the news going on in 1938-39, or the beginnings of the 40s, Pearl Harbor and all...."

The announcer on "So Goes the World"—we'd call him the anchorman these days—was probably Seattle's most commanding news personality of all time. His name was Dick Keplinger.

Speaking in a rich, friendly but authoritative baritone, Keplinger was for years news and special events director for KOMO-KJR. His evening straight-news shows were sponsored by Shell Oil and got top ratings.

"Kep" was at his best, though, when reporting on-the-spot events. Kidnappings, the Tacoma Narrows Bridge collapse, and V-J Day were typically grist for the Keplinger mill.

Probably the most paradoxical broadcast Kep ever made was when he drove to Boeing Field and interviewed half-a-dozen Japanese making a round-the-world "good will" tour. Not long afterward came the attack on Pearl Harbor and the United States' entry into the war.

Keplinger joined the Army and after several false starts (they wanted to make a baker or truck driver out of him) Kep wound up as announcer for the "Army Hour" program, criss-crossing the nation with the Army Band and selling war bonds.

After the war he returned to Seattle as a free-lance announcer, often originating his programs from a studio in his own home in the Washington Park district of Seattle. He had his own teletype machines there and used to broadcast the news in his shorts, while family members wandered in and out with fruit juice and snacks.

In 1943, Keplinger won the prestigious H. P. Davis National Memorial award as America's top announcer.

Kep's career was tragically foreshortened, however, ending abruptly with his death in 1965 at age fifty.

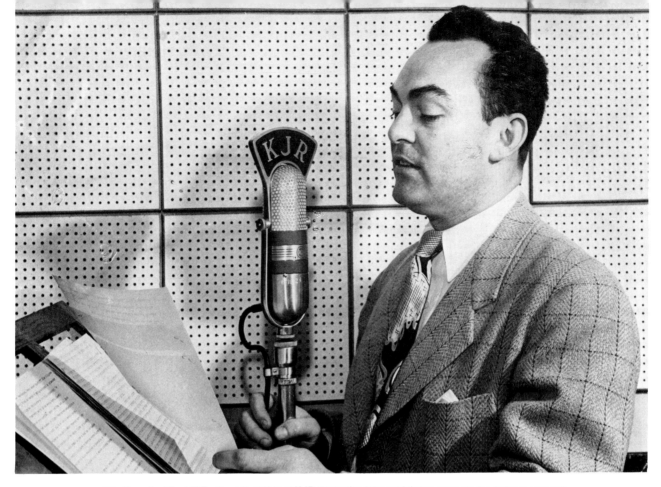

"So Goes the World!" Each week actors at **KJR** dramatized the world's top news stories, in the manner of Time magazine's "The March of Time." News and Special Events Director **Dick Keplinger** announced the local series. His delivery was only slightly less sepulchral than that with which Westbrook Van Voorhis, his famous counterpart on the network version, assured us that "Time…marches on!"

In the photo below, **Keplinger** (center, with **KJR** mike) interviews visiting around-the-world "good will tour" of Japanese at Boeing Field. The event preceded by a short time the attack on Pearl Harbor which launched the U.S. into World War 2.

KJR's news staff as the war got underway. From left: **Bob Ackerley**, **Dick Keplinger**, and **Bob Ferris**.
Below: crowds jammed "Victory Square" (University Street between Fourth and Fifth in Seattle) for daily noontime broadcasts of entertainment, speeches and war bond sales.

"Clifford and Clark" were an institution on Seattle radio stations for more than 30 years. The keyboard artistries of organist **Eddie Clifford** (top) and pianist **Freeman "Tubby" Clark** were also featured over Channel 5 in TV's early days.

Dramatic "cue music" for "So Goes the World" (and many other programs) was played by Freeman "Tubby" Clark. Clark, whose generous heft once justified that nickname (it doesn't any more) was later teamed on piano with organist Eddie Clifford in a musical partnership that was to last some twenty-five years. The enormously popular duo not only played and chatted over the air each day, but entertained evenings at the Olympic Hotel's Marine Room for so many years, they were practically fixtures.

That wasn't Tubby's first time at the Olympic, by the way. He was barely out of Ballard High when, in 1933, he was hired to play piano with a dance orchestra

there. It was directed by the future radio announcer, Wendell Niles.

"Clifford and Clark" were heard over various stations but would reach their pinnacle of popularity during the war years on KIRO. By then they had a repertoire of some two thousand songs, which they mostly played without rehearsals, just cueing each other with nods and some special kind of ESP.

KIRO was an old Seattle station, remarkably reborn. It had been founded back in 1927 as KPCB by Moritz Thomsen, head of the **P**acific **C**oast **B**iscuit Company. Thomsen also owned the Centennial Flour Mills of

Chet Huntley, future TV newsman, was a poorly paid announcer for **KPCB**, Seattle, in 1934. Here he produces a one-man low-budget "opera broadcast" using phonograph albums, sound effect records of applause and the orchestra's tuning up, and his own commentary.

Seattle, which was the Fisher company's principal rival. KPCB was supposed to be Centennial's answer to KOMO.

But the little 100-watt station never made much of a splash. That it is remembered at all these days is largely because of a certain struggling, square-jawed University student, hired as an announcer there in 1934. He was Chet Huntley.

Huntley only earned fifteen dollars a month cash, but he was permitted—encouraged, really—to slip in free plugs for restaurants and hotels which gave him meals and lodging in return. Later, he and Trevor Evans shared expenses in a bachelor's apartment, and teamed up to do book review programs on the station. (There was no pay involved—just all the free books they could read.)

Of course times were hard all over, but even allowing for the Depression, KPCB's poverty was the joke of the industry. Once when a stationery store cut off the station's credit, the staff bought paper, pencils and other supplies out of their own pockets. And the equipment kept breaking down, because the station couldn't afford parts to make permanent repairs.

Naturally KPCB couldn't afford a wire service. Part of Huntley's job, therefore, was to buy a Seattle paper on the way to work each day, and rewrite the main stories into a fifteen-minute newscast. He could scarcely have guessed where this modest start in the news business would lead him.

Huntley was from the buffalo grass country of Montana, the son of a railroad telegrapher. He had wanted to be a doctor, not a broadcaster; though he had once "announced" World Series games to a group of townspeople, reading out the ticker reports his father intercepted down at the depot.

From Seattle Chet went to KHQ in Spokane for a time, then KGW, Portland, and finally to Los Angeles, where he wound up announcing late evening news opposite Sam Hayes, NBC's enormously popular Richfield Reporter. Later he was lured back east where, eventually, NBC teamed him with David Brinkley in the award-winning news programs that dominated TV in the late fifties and early sixties.

Huntley had just been at KPCB a year or so when that station was sold to a determined Seattle businessman-politician, Saul Haas. (It's pronounced "Hass.")

Haas was a towering figure in many ways. A large and complex man with puffy eyes and Richard Nixon jowls. A wheeler-dealer who acknowledged no obstacles—but suffered exquisite feelings of personal insecurity. An irresistible force, compulsively chewing up immovable objects for dinner.

Saul Haas had tasted poverty as a boy in New York's lower East Side. He came West and taught school briefly, oddly enough at both Yale and Harvard, which happen to be small towns in Idaho. Then he went into newspapering, managing two Pacific Northwest papers (one of which went broke) before turning to politics and broadcasting. For a time he was president of a small Seattle investment company.

Haas was not popular with many investors, nor with his fellow radio tycoons. In industries that were top-heavy with Republicans, his sin was to be an ardent Democrat. In 1932 he had managed Homer T. Bone's run for the United States Senate. And Bone, a longtime champion of labor and social reform, was a whole-hearted supporter of Presidential candidate Franklin Roosevelt.

Both candidates won, and Haas was rewarded with appointment as Collector of Customs at Seattle. He held that office until 1946.

Haas had his first brush with broadcasting in 1931 when he was appointed receiver for one of Hi Pierce's bankrupt stock companies. His job: to try and recover $300,000 allegedly siphoned into the running of KJR. He may not have gotten the money, but he did get to know something of the business of radio. Later he became acquainted with Moritz Thomsen through some sort of row Thomsen's son was having with the U.S. Customs. Haas wound up buying a piece of

Bill Reuter, announcer-operator for the Pacific Coast Biscuit Co. station **KPCB** (later **KIRO**) in 1932. The station is still using an old-fashioned Western Electric double-button carbon microphone in this picture.

Note the looseleaf notebook containing commercials and such gems of "continuity" as: "That was Ruth Etting with the Columbia Recording Orchestra who just dropped by to ask the musical question, 'What Wouldn't I Do For That Man.'"

KPCB about 1933, and gained control of the station a couple of years later.

Haas changed the call letters to KIRO and raised the station's power to 500 watts. But he was still hampered by money problems. KIRO was so lacking in equipment at first that after a remote broadcast, they would have to play record music while the station's few microphones were rushed back to the studio by taxicab.

After a year of hard work, KIRO was actually turning a modest profit. But Haas had set his sights high. What he really wanted was to make his station the most powerful and influential voice in the Pacific Northwest. He wanted a distinguished network. And he wanted relicensing to high power on an interference-free "clear channel" frequency. And of course, he got it all.

In another year the newly created FCC—the seven commissioners were Roosevelt appointees, after all—assigned him 1,000 watts on 710 kilocycles, a frequency he shared only with WOR in Newark, New Jersey. With this leverage he was able to woo CBS away from KOL, and later from KVI. (These stations kept their Don Lee affiliation and KOL subsequently added a new network called the Mutual Broadcasting System.*)

KIRO was the first station in the Pacific Northwest to be licensed all the way up to 50,000 watts of power. This took place in June, 1941, and before any other station in the area could follow suit, World War Two came along and the Commission froze all station construction, including power increases. KIRO thus remained the most powerful radio voice north of San Francisco and west of Minneapolis until after the war.

Which didn't hurt the balance sheets of either KIRO or Saul Haas, you may be sure.

* Mutual began on the East Coast in the early thirties as a three-station hookup sharing a single program: "The Lone Ranger."

Seattle broadcasting magnate and politician **Saul Haas** (left) turned an all but bankrupt **KPCB** into **KIRO**, one of the area's most influential and powerful radio stations. Here he chats with the famous newscaster-explorer, **Lowell Thomas**, about 1955.

"Women in Defense" was one of the hundreds of war-effort programs and series broadcast by Seattle stations during the war. Here broadcaster **Alice Emel** poses in the uniform of a Civil Defense volunteer.

KIRO's trademark was a relaxed announcing style that contrasted pleasantly with the big, formal sound other network stations tried for. On the breaks between programs, announcers identified it as "The Friendly Station."

Saul Haas was legendary from Washington State to Washington, D.C. as a two-fisted drinker who consumed whiskey by the pint without showing the effects. But a time came when Haas' boozing ceased to amuse and amaze. He fought his bottle battle with valor, winning it in the end; but for a time there were some lost skirmishes which dealt big trouble to the KIRO crew.

Haas had the habit, when in his cups, of calling up the station and talking at length to the announcers on duty. There were frequent fatherly monologues of the By-George-but-you're-lucky-to-be-working-for-me theme. And there were certain people he routinely and vehemently fired (only to rehire them, with not even a bland apology, next day).

One night shortly after the nation entered the war, while Bruce Calhoun was announcing a midnight concert, Haas phoned and directed Calhoun to write a news story attacking William Randolph Hearst. Of course Haas and the powerful Republican magnate were on opposite political wavelengths and their

KIRO's transmitter building on Vashon Island was completed shortly before Pearl Harbor was attacked in 1941. Owner Saul Haas, determined to keep the station on the air in case the war came to Puget Sound, had the 120-foot cedar pole erected behind the building as an emergency antenna tower. Windows were fitted with strong screens for protection against bombing and antiaircraft fire. Still later a fall-out shelter was added when developments posed the threat of atomic war.

enmity was nothing novel. But Calhoun was stunned. Haas wanted Hearst "exposed" as a Nazi and a traitor, consciously working to undermine America's war effort.

Calhoun wrote a story and read it on the air, but Haas wasn't satisfied. "Do it again," he said, "and make it stronger!" So Calhoun did, praying for once nobody was listening. But somebody was, and next morning the P-I (a Hearst newspaper) was angrily demanding Haas' scalp.

They didn't get it. Haas had too many friends in too high places. Friends like Treasury Secretary Henry Morgenthau, and Justice William O. Douglas, and a

Bruce Calhoun's was a familiar voice in the 40's. As a freelancer he made as many as 49 different broadcasts a week on various Pacific Northwest stations. Calhoun later worked for the University of Washington where he battled for the concept of public broadcasting, leading finally to the establishment of **KUOW** and **KCTS**, Channel 9.

Al Schuss, who started in radio at **KJR** in the 20's, changed his name to Alan Hale when he hit the big time. Here's Al broadcasting coast-to-coast from the Rock Island Arsenal in Illinois during the war.

(University of Washington)

Shortly after President Roosevelt named him to a Supreme Court vacancy, **William O. Douglas** inscribed this jubilant photo to his old friend, Saul Haas. Haas, a Democratic Party power at the time, is credited with engineering Douglas' appointment.

(CBS News)

A very young **Edward R. Murrow** poses with CBS microphone, scratch pad, and ever-present cigarette.

Murrow grew up in northwest Washington, studied radio speech at Washington State College. As CBS' chief European correspondent during the war, he virtually invented broadcast journalism as it is known today.

slender young politician from Texas named Lyndon Johnson.

In his autobiography, *Go East, Young Man*, Douglas recalls with affection the hunting and fishing expeditions he shared with Saul Haas. He even credits Haas with engineering his 1939 appointment to the Supreme Court.

Douglas' book also recounts a classic incident said to have occurred during KIRO's early days. It seems the station's early-morning announcer arrived for work badly hung over. He signed the station on the air and introduced the day's first program, a quarter-hour religious offering on a 16-inch long-playing disc (they were called "electrical transcriptions" then). Then he absented himself long enough to visit a corner coffee shop and grab a badly needed cuppa joe, black.

Returning to the station about twelve minutes later he found the switchboard aflame with incoming phone calls, and the needle stuck in one of the first grooves of the fifteen-minute E.T. The radio preacher had barely gotten started on his opening prayer, and was saying over and over, "Oh Jesus Christ, Oh Jesus Christ, Oh Jesus...."

The most prominent Northwest broadcaster to be heard regularly on KIRO never worked for the station. Edward R. Murrow's "This...is London" wartime broadcasts were carried nationwide over CBS, elevating radio news to new plateaus of impactful immediacy.

Murrow grew up on the Samish Flats south of Bellingham, and in 1926 went off to attend Washington State College in Pullman. W.S.C. had the nation's first college-level courses in broadcasting, and one of the first campus radio stations, a pioneer 500-watter with the call letters KWSC.

Besides radio speech, Ed studied drama and debating, while working part-time at the station. He did an occasional sportscast, but mostly he read agricultural extension bulletins on the air. They bored him, and a co-worker recalled that he didn't always show up for his shift.

Ten years later, Murrow *was* at just the right place and time, as European director of CBS. Not quite as big a deal as it sounds, to begin with, since most overseas feeds then were folk song festivals, wine carnivals, bird calls and the like. But he was on the spot when Europe began "tearing up its maps," as he put it, and the rest is radio history.

But Murrow almost didn't get to make those famous rooftop broadcasts of the London bombings. Air Ministry censors wouldn't allow him to broadcast live, for fear of giving the Germans too-timely information. Seven times he and a technician braved the bombs to make dramatic sample recordings, which proved quite acceptable to the censors; but CBS refused to air them due to the ban on records.

Finally Ed appealed to Winston Churchill himself for permission to do live broadcasts and the Prime Minister, who turned out to be a great Murrow fan, readily agreed.

"This...is London!" **Ed Murrow**'s wartime reports to America described the horror and heroism of England's "finest hour" under the Nazi blitz. Here Murrow crosses a rainy London street in June, 1941, as BBC's Broadcast House looms in the background.

By D-Day the no-records rule had been sensibly relaxed so correspondents could get stories unobtainable otherwise. One of the most spectacular was Murrow's first-hand account of Allied airborne troops being dropped into German-occupied Holland. (Ed had been ordered repeatedly not to go on offensive missions, but he would buckle on his flak suit and go just the same.) You could even hear the graphic snap of lashings as the troopers hooked up to the static line, and their fading shouts as they fell away from the plane, one by one.

Local outlets were using records by now too, but the results were not always so splendid.

KIRO once sent a team to the Bremerton Navy Yard to cover the dedication of a new aircraft carrier. A very high-ranking dignitary made the commissioning speech, which they recorded for later broadcast. They used a heavy glass-base disc, and nobody noticed it kept slowing down during the recording.

When the record was played on the air that evening, the sound of course came off faster and faster, and higher and higher pitched, so that the distinguished admiral seemed to segue from a serious war-effort speech into a first-rate imitation of Donald Duck.

Len Beardsley, the announcer on duty, could think of no way to slow the disc down, of course. Anyway he was too busy laughing and trying to placate the enraged naval officer, who was on the phone and chewing out with awesome eloquence the radio station, its personnel, and its equipment.

Broadcasting nationwide on "The Army Hour," Seattle's **Dick Keplinger** describes a new 60-mm. knee mortar. Sept. 17, 1944, was the date.

On the Air

These programs are compiled from radio stations' latest data. THE POST-INTELLIGENCER assumes no responsibility for last-minute program changes or cancellations due to war orders.

FRIDAY, OCTOBER 30

A. M.	KIRO—710 KC.	KOMO—950 KC.	A. M.	KJR—1000 KC.	KOL—1300 KC.
7:00	News	News	7:00	nEveryman's Chapel	nNews
7:15	Farm Forum	Top O' The Morning	7:15	News	nHappy Johnny
7:30	Dick Joy; News	nReveille Roundup	7:30	nBreakfast Club	nNews
7:45	Norman Runions	nSam Hayes, News	7:45	" Don McNeill	Sacred Heart
8:00	Man About Town	Radio Parade	8:00	Everyman's Chapel	nBreakfast Club
8:15	News	News	8:15	nRoy Porter	" (Continued)
8:30	nValiant Lady	Victor Lindlahr	8:30	nBreakfast Club	News
8:45	nStories America Loves	nDavid Harum	8:45	Unity Viewpoint	Musicale
9:00	nKate Smith Speaks	nThe O'Neills	9:00	News	nBoake Carter
9:15	nBig Sister	Good News Time	9:15	A Woman Wonders	Ray Daughters
9:30	nHelen Trent Romance	nTed Steele	9:30	nBreakfast at Sardi's	KOL Album; music
9:45	nOur Gal Sunday	Novelty Time	9:45	" (Continued)	Arizona Joe
10:00	nLife Can Be Beautiful	nR. Walker's Kitchen	10:00	nBaukhage Talking	nNews, Hardy
10:15	nMa Perkins	News	10:15	nLittle Jack Little	We the Women
10:30	nVic and Sade	Musical Jewel Box	10:30	Benny Walker	News, Political
10:45	nThe Goldbergs	nDr. Kate	10:45	" (Continued)	Political Talk
11:00	nYoung Dr. Malone	nLight of the World	11:00	nNancy Martin, Songs	Political Talk
11:15	nAunt Jenny's Stories	nLonely Women	11:15	Between the Bookends	Betty Lou Shops
11:30	nWe Love and Learn	nGuiding Light	11:30	News	Political Talk
11:45	U. S. Navy	nBetty Crocker	11:45	Cowboy Joe	Short Story

P. M.	KIRO—710 KC.	KOMO—950 KC. Afternoon		KJR—1000 KC.	KOL—1300 KC.
12:00	Radio Today; Songs	nMary Marlin	12:00	nPrescott Presents	News
12:15	nNews; Bob Andersen	nMa Perkins	12:15	" (Continued)	Christian Business
12:30	nJoyce Jordan, M. D.	nPepper Young Family	12:30	nMen of Sea	" Men's Committee
12:45	nBachelor's Children	nRight to Happiness	12:45	Deane Dickason	nPhiladelphia Symph'y.
1:00	Galen Drake	nBackstage Wife	1:00	nClub Matinee	" (Continued)
1:15	nSam Hayes, News	nStella Dallas	1:15	Cecil Solly	KOL Album
1:30	nAmerican School	nLorenzo Jones	1:30	nClub Matinee	nN. Y. Racing Program
1:45	" Bellingham H. S.	nYoung Widder Brown	1:45	" (Continued); News	Melody Supplement
2:00	Housewives, Inc.	nWhen a Girl Marries	2:00	nClancy Calling	nSheelah Carter
2:15	" (Continued)	nPortia Faces Life	2:15	" (Continued)	nNewsreel Theater
2:30	nWm. Winter, News	nJust Plain Bill	2:30	nUnannounced	n " (Continued)
2:45	nBen Bernie	nFront Page Farrell.	2:45	Sing Me a Song	n " (Continued)
3:00	Art Lindsay	nRoad of Life	3:00	News	nNtl. Pryr.;P.K.Gordon
3:15	nHedda Hopper	nVic and Sade	3:15	Serenade	Music, Political
3:30	nKeep Singing, America	nAgainst the Storm	3:30	nGospel Singer	Starred For Listening
3:45	nThe World Today	nJudy and Jane	3:45	Music; Goodwill	Music; nNews
4:00	nSecond Mrs. Burton	Home Calendar	4:00	nScramble	nFulton Lewis Jr.
4:15	Newsreel	" (Continued)	4:15	" Drama	nJohnson Family
4:30	nEasy Aces	nChas. Dant Orch.	4:30	Parents and Children	Playgrounds; music
4:45	Mr. Keen	nOrgan	4:45	nNews	Treasury Star Parade
5:00	Initiative 151	Transitunes	5:00	nDon Winslow, navy	News—H'w'd Costigan
5:15	" (Cont'd.); Stanislo	News	5:15	Sea Hound	Starred for Listening
5:30	Evening Almanac	Folk Music	5:30	nJack Armstrong	For Initiative 151
5:45	nTrum'n Bradley, News	nBy The Way	5:45	nCaptain Midnight	" (Continued)

P. M.	KIRO—710 KC.	KOMO—950 KC. Evening		KJR—1000 KC.	KOL—1300 KC.
6:00	Tonight at Fort Lewis	nWaltz Time	6:00	nHop Harrigan	nGabriel Heatter
6:15	" (Continued)	" (Continued)	6:15	News	News; nJim Doyle
6:30	nThat Brewster Boy	nPlantation Party	6:30	nSpotlight Bands	nState and War
6:45	" (Continued)	" Variety Show	6:45	" (Continued); Skit	Political Talk
7:00	nCaravan	nPeople Are Funny	7:00	nMeet Your Navy	Boxing Bout
7:15	" Jack Pearl	" (Continued)	7:15	" (Continued)	" (Continued)
7:30	" (Continued)	nTommy Riggs and	7:30	This Is Magic	" (Continued)
7:45	" (Continued)	" Betty Lou	7:45	nMen, Machines	" (Continued)
8:00	nAmos and Andy	nPleasure Time	8:00	nWatch World Go By	Lone Ranger
8:15	nMoylen Sisters	News Reporter	8:15	nDinah Shore	" (Continued)
8:30	nPlayhouse	nWhodunit	8:30	nGang Busters	Musical Interlude
8:45	"Melvyn Douglas	" (Continued)	8:45	" (Continued)	For Referendum 22
9:00	nKate Smith	nInterlude; Dance	9:00	Fishfinder	nNews; Hardy
9:15	" Janet Blair	Standby America	9:15	Standby America	Carroll Carter
9:30	" Hazel Scott	Army Recruiting	9:30	News Reporter	nJohn B. Hughes
9:45	" (Continued)	Chris Gilson	9:45	Norman Sper	nFulton Lewis Jr.
10:00	nOur Secret Weapon	nReporter News	10:00	Fireside Meditations	Arizona Joe
10:15	News Roundup	Starlight Souvenirs	10:15	" (Continued)	News Review
10:30	" (Continued)	nDance Orchestra	10:30	Gospel Hour	nSymphony
10:45	Political Forum	" (Continued); News	10:45	" (Continued)	" (Continued)
11:00	" (Continued)	Evening Reveries	11:00	nFolk Music	Dance Time
11:15	Civilian Protection	" (Continued)	11:15	" (Continued)	Starred for Listening
11:30	War Chest	nUncle Sam Presents	11:30	Melody Lane	nFireside Melodies
11:45	News for Alaska	nNews	11:45	nOrgan	" (Continued)
12:00	Concert; continuous	Silent	12:00	Continuous programs	Silent

nDesignates network programs; KIRO on CBS; KOMO on NBC; KJR on BNC; KOL-KMO on MBS, MDL.

KIRO Highlights
2:00 p. m.—Housewives, Inc.
4:30 p. m.—Easy Aces.

THE 'BAER' FACTS

THE PHANTOM

MICKEY MOUSE

FLASH GORDON

TIM TYLER'S LUCK

This is what you could hear on Seattle's network stations back in October, 1942. Note frequent war effort and news shows mingling with soap operas, live music and radio plays.

Bruce Calhoun, **Gordon Tuell**, **Bob Berry** and **Murray Boggs** of **KIRO** setting up for a remote broadcast of the "Mr. Wyde-Awake" quiz show in a Seattle theater.

Tape recording was a German invention and didn't come into use here until after the war,* but U.S. stations made some use of similar apparatus using spools of wire. KIRO wire-recorded the maiden flight of Boeing's first swept-wing bomber, picking up the takeoff roar and the tower operator's dramatic chatter, for delayed broadcast. Back at the station, and after a great deal of advance ballyhoo for the show, the wire suddenly flew off its reel in a hundred different directions.

Nothing left but a tangle of loops and kinks.

There was no salvaging the recording so three or four staffers secretly re-created the entire broadcast, using sound effects and muffling the "tower operator's" voice through a waste paper basket. Nobody ever knew the difference.

Not until now, anyway.

Between Boeing and the shipyards, Puget Sound was heavily involved in the war, and local stations

* The big German recorders were mounted in trucks. The author was at AFN Frankfurt, key station for the American forces' broadcasting net in Europe just after the war, where a captured machine was used for routine news coverage—possibly a first for American broadcasters.

were airing a great many shows for the defense effort. Sergeant Howard Duff, stationed at Fort Lewis, came by to help his home town put on some of the programs. Many of them were written by Duff's old friend and scripter from "Junior G-Men" days, Trevor Evans, in a series called "Our State at War."

Evans had meanwhile become radio director for a large ad agency, and was always looking for fresh talent. One day "Jamie" Jamieson, whose popular show reported Seattle's waterfront doings, asked if he'd ever heard of Ivar Haglund. He hadn't.

Haglund ran a little hole-in-the-wall aquarium down on the waterfront. You got in for twelve cents and a trained seal named Pat splashed joyfully when you paid.

To promote the aquarium, Haglund had bought a weekly quarter hour of cheap radio time on a local station. To a twangy guitar accompaniment he rendered good-natured folk songs, interspersed with fishy little jingles of his own about "Halley the Halibut," "Oscar the Octopus," "Hermie the Hermit Crab" and so on. Haglund had a rare sense of humor, and his program—if not quite great music—was at least great fun.

Evans caught the show and liked it so much, he sold Haglund five-days-a-week to a sponsor who hadn't even heard him.

At the end of the first week Evans phoned his client and asked what he thought of the program.

"It stinks," said the sponsor. "Cancel it."

Evans was still trying to think how to break this news to Ivar when the client called back. He wanted to know how much mail his programs usually received.

"Oh, people don't write fan letters any more," Evans told him, and named a modest number of letters for the past year.

"Well," the sponsor told him, "You'd better keep this Haglund guy on. We got that many so far this week."

Haglund's program, "Around the Sound," had a ten-year run over KJR and, later, KIRO. Ivar saved the money he made in radio and used it to open the first of a string of restaurants in 1946. He named it "Acres of Clams" after his radio theme song.

Haglund's ingenious gimmicks for promoting his eateries are a Seattle legend. His motto became "Keep clam." His "ever-rejuvenating clam nectar" was sold subject to a three-cup limit (absolutely no exceptions!) to "any married man, without written permission of his wife."

Ivar once invited "Two Ton" Tony Galento, the grunt-and-groaner, to wrestle Oscar, his octopus. He held yearly clam-eating contests. And at Christmas time, he used to take his pet seal up to Frederick & Nelson to see Santa Claus.

Another long-time institution on Seattle radio was Cecil Solly, the gardening expert. Solly was from Canterbury, England, and sounded like it. His career over KJR, KIRO and practically every other station

(University of Washington)

Sergeant **Howard Duff** was stationed at Fort Lewis for a time during World War 2 and appeared in radio shows connected with the war effort. Duff was a graduate of Roosevelt High School and was once a staff announcer for **KOMO-KJR**. He later gained fame as a radio and screen actor and starred with his wife Ida Lupino in an early TV comedy, "Mr. Adams and Eve."

"This tape will self-destruct...!" Seattle's **Steven Hill** played Dan Briggs, head of the original "Mission Impossible" team on TV. Hill, whose real name is Saul Krakovski, was a **KOMO** announcer in the early 40's. His first acting parts were in war effort scripts written by Trevor Evans.

Stephen E. Sanislo was a young Seattle Fire Department captain when **KFOA** asked him to help put on a skit about fire prevention. That was in 1924. Sanislo was such a hit the broadcast was repeated twice, and he devoted the rest of his life to talking about fire safety. His thousands of broadcasts were never dull, being peppered with humor and sound effects—fire sirens, crackling flames, barking dogs and the like—all of which he did himself.

Sanislo was a true celebrity in Seattle, where generations of children were entertained as he visited their schools, wearing his uniform and an animated smile, and preaching good citizenship.

To my old home town, Seattle, and all the a + Ra gang—my very best wishes. Bill Gavin

Announcer **Bill Gavin** doubled as music director for Captain Dobbsie and others. After some years with **KOMO**, his talent led him to California and the "big time."

on Puget Sound spanned 36 years and some 20,000 broadcasts. "Country Gardens" was the theme of his daily show, on which he dispensed the last word in dependable horticultural information for Pacific Northwesterners.

Solly took his broadcasting seriously. Once in 1934 a forest fire broke out on his farm, north of Seattle. He joined firefighters battling the blaze until twenty minutes before broadcast time, then with flames licking almost at his doorstep, drove off at top speed to do his daily show.

He arrived at the studio with seconds to spare, his face and clothes caked with smoke, grime and sweat.

Then after fifteen minutes' calm discourse on the proper bedding of weak-stemmed petunias, Solly sped back to help save his farm from destruction.

Versatile **Bob Hurd** was a talented announcer, actor, writer and producer of radio shows. When TV came along he even turned model and appeared in clothing ads. This is Bob back in radio days on **KOMO**.

SOUND: Ship's bells and whistle.
MATE: "All ashore that's going ashore!"
THEME: "Ship ahoy! Ship ahoy! Oh, we're sailing the Ship of Joy, Sailor Boy!
    Pack your grip and wave a kiss, it's a trip you shouldn't miss...."

Hugh Barrett Dobbs was "Captain Dobbsie," an 8 a.m. institution on the Pacific Coast from radio's very early days. Originally a physical culture instructor and a designer of school playgrounds for U.S. cities (including Seattle) he did a pioneering early-morning exercise program for San Francisco's **KPO**. It went over so well Shell Oil signed him to emcee a daily hour of music, poetry and good thoughts built around a mythical cruise "from Good Cheer Dock to the Isles of Happiness." Six stations carried the program until 1939 when Dobbs brought it to Seattle and **KOMO** fed the "Ship of Joy" to a smaller network of Northwest outlets.

A highlight of each day's progam was the Wishing Well ceremony. Dobbs would ask everyone to stand, place right hand over heart, and "send out a wish to somebody—somewhere—who may be in sickness or trouble." Then as he commanded: "Everybody—WISH!" listeners were to throw their right arms "high into the air in a vast wave of good will."

Dobbsie's sign-off was equally sentimental: "And now, Shipmates, with hand at salute I wish you Godspeed. May your hopes reach fruition. May blessings shower you. May Happiness keep your skies radiant. For you—and you—and you—wherever you are, whoever you are, HA-A-A-PY DA-A-A-Y!!"

(Seattle Times)

(3-M Co.)

In 1947 Seattle's famous tenor, **Lanny Ross**, made history of sorts by singing on the first program to be taped by ten recorders at one time. The experiment (shown here) was carried on at St. Paul, Minnesota by the makers of now-famous "Scotch" recording tape. A year later Bing Crosby made the big breakthrough, switching from live to pre-taped performances, thus ending the networks' longtime insistence on live broadcasts exclusively.

Oscar Marcos Jorgenson was the "Scandinavian Reporter." His daily program in Norwegian was a long-time fixture on Northwest radio. It finally succumbed to a World War 2 ban on foreign language broadcasts.

A consistently popular singer on Seattle radio was Hugh Poore, a short, fleshy Alabaman who went by the name of "Cowboy Joe." Joe began on KJR in the twenties, and was still doing a daily quarter hour of rather soulful guitar-accompanied folk and Western ditties some two decades further down the trail.

Cowboy Joe had a phenomenal memory and was said to know over a thousand songs by heart. A poll of Northwest fans once selected him as radio's top vocalist, even beating out such famous singers as Bing Crosby and John Charles Thomas.

And then there was Oscar Marcos Jorgenson.

By day, Jorgenson was a mild-mannered suit salesman for the Lundquist Lilly store. But late each afternoon he would hike up Fifth to the Skinner Building, and duck into a radio booth to become— The Scandinavian Reporter.

Jorgenson had learned Norwegian and Swedish as a boy in Minnesota, and with these languages he reported the day's events for Scandinavian listeners all over the Northwest. His 6 p.m. program was heard over KXA at first, later switching to KJR, continuing for some twenty years in all. The show went off the air in World War II when foreign languages were banned from the airwaves.

Jorgenson's program began with a few bars of "Swedish Wedding Bells" and a salutation that sounded like "Good aften, gut fok."

Which was the cue for us non-Scandihoovian listeners to tune in something else.

One year the Fisher stations got a new advertising manager who began expounding on program changes he wanted to make.

"The first thing," he growled, "is to get rid of that damned Scandinavian."

Gently, staffers suggested he check the program's Hooper rating first. The Puget Sound country, he learned, was teeming with Swedes and Norwegians who were loyal tuners-in. It seems that in those days, "that damned Scandinavian" had more listeners than almost anything else on the air.

Male quartets were very big on radio throughout the medium's "golden years." Here (left to right) **Hal Wallis**, **Wesley Ebey**, **Phil Wacker** and **George Peckham** make with the Jingle Bells during the Christmas season of 1947, on **KIRO**.

"**KOL** Carnival" was a daily extravaganza of live music, fun and nonsense broadcast during that station's best years—a heyday that began April 9, 1930 when Paul Whiteman's band helped open new, spacious studios in the Northern Life Tower (now the Seattle Tower). The station began to wind down after 1936 when Saul Haas' **KIRO** lured away **KOL**'s affiliation with CBS.

Pictured here, standing, from left: **Frank Anderson**, **Paul McCrea**, **Alex Forbes**, **Glen Eaton**, **Arthur Butler**, **Mark Rowan**, **Bill Arndt**, and **Wendell Niles**. Seated: "**Arizona Joe**," **Helene Hill**, **Helen Greco** (who later became Mrs. Spike Jones), **Ken Stuart**, **Ivan Ditmars**, and **Billie Lowe**.

Wheeler Smith's calm delivery over **KOL** in the 40's never changed, whether he was announcing a world crisis or just the latest "swing" tune. Always relaxed, Smith could be chatting here with a friend while awaiting the cue to broadcast.

Note the buzzer, bell and batteries outfit used for sound effects on some programs.

Bob Nichols and **Lola Hallowell** broadcasting a "Where to go in Seattle" sequence on Nichols' afternoon show for Best's Apparel, about 1946. Lola now operates her own talent and model agency in Seattle.

Ruth McCloy and **Dick Keplinger** enjoying an interview with **Art Linkletter** on the "Ruth and Dick" show, about 1952.

CHAPTER SEVEN

KING's Kameras

We tend to think of television as a fairly recent invention. Actually, its origins go back to the earliest days of radio—and before.

The basic invention was the scanning wheel, devised in 1884 by a German, Paul Nipkow. Around the edges of this primitive device was a shallow spiral of tiny holes. When the disc was spun in front of a picture, the holes successively "scanned" the image, producing a single continuous series of light and dark impulses.

These impulses could then be converted to electrical signals for transmission. They were sent over wires in early experiments, but radio would have worked just as well.

Marconi was confidently predicting "visible telephone" by wireless as far back as 1915. And just following the first World War, with radio broadcasting yet to break away from the garages and basements of hobbyists like Vincent Kraft, European experimenters were already transmitting pictures through the air.

But unlike radio, television signals could not be picked up with a galena crystal and a few cents worth of wire. TV receivers were complicated. The scanning disc at the sending end, for example, had to have its counterpart at the receiver, and there was a nightmare of mechanics involved in getting the discs to turn synchronously. Meanwhile mere radio was capturing the awed attention of the public, broadcasters, industry and government alike.

Sound without wires seemed miracle enough. There was no great hurry to add pictures.

By 1928, though, a few eastern stations were experimenting with TV. WGY, Schenectady, transmitted history's first television play that year.

And on June 3, 1929, TV pictures were broadcast in Seattle for the first time ever.

It wasn't much of a program—mostly simple figures like a heart, diamond, question mark, letters and numbers. Not much audience either: a handful of people gathered around crude, home-made sets with one-inch screens.

That pioneer experiment was the work of Francis J. Brott, chief engineer for KOMO. There was a feeling that television was just around the corner, and Brott wanted the Fisher station to be first with the new medium.

Just before the historic tests were to start, though, a power supply tube blew out in Brott's gear. He hastily borrowed a replacement supply from his friend, Palmer Leberman. Leberman owned a rather insignificant little 50-watt station that played records all day. Its call letters were KRSC.

Neither man could know there would in fact be two decades of Depression and World War before the introduction of commercial TV in the Northwest, and that the first station on the air with pictures would not be KOMO, the big Fisher station, but Leberman's KRSC.

Sandy-haired Palmer K. Leberman stood tall and ramrod straight, as he had learned in Naval Academy days. Already he looked every inch the distinguished businessman he would become later on, when he made his mark in New York, publishing Family Circle magazine. In 1927, though, he was just another radio buff, tinkering with a home-built "rig" in the basement of his Lake Washington home. The call letters stood for "Kelvinator Radio Sales Corporation," the name of a small appliance store Leberman ran downtown at Fifth and University.

Here's Television---He Sends, She Receives

Seeing was believing for the radio amateur fraternity last evening when F. J. Brott, prominent Seattle radio engineer, inaugurated television broadcasting. At left, Brott is shown at his transmitter. The motion picture projection machine flashes an image on a scanning disc. Photoelectric cells change the light impulses into electric impulses and the picture is broadcast.

Mary Lawrence, 1149 Thirty-third Avenue North, points to the picture as it is seen at the receiving end. The box-like affair contains the necessary apparatus for reception, including a motor, a scanning disc and a neon lamp. The image, in colors, forms on a plate approximately one inch square.

PLANE ALASKA | 1,200 SENIORS | Rookie Aviators | YAKIMA HIKERS

June 4, 1929 Seattle P-I tells of the area's first television transmissions, broadcast the day before by **KOMO** chief engineer **Francis Brott**. The tiny picture, scarcely more than an inch square, even had "color:" rather than black and white, the images showed up red on a white background.

KRSC eventually moved to Seattle's Henry Building for a couple of years, and then struggled through the thirties from a small room atop the Washington Athletic Club.

Back east, experimental television was struggling too. But by 1939 a scattering of viewers could see President Roosevelt open the World's Fair in New York, and they could watch a few selected sports events. The following year, both Democratic and Republican national conventions were televised for the very first time.

Daily TV programs (two or three hours a day on half a dozen eastern stations) began in 1941, but it didn't matter much because right away the war started, and there were no more receivers being built.

When the shooting stopped there was more delay while the FCC pondered new technical rules. Meanwhile, Palmer Leberman's enterprising urges led him to establish KRSC-FM, the Puget Sound country's first frequency-modulation station, ushering in a new era of clean, high-fidelity broadcast sound.

Engineers had scarcely finished debugging the FM transmitter when Leberman also announced plans for KRSC-TV. It was to be the fifteenth television station in the United States, and the first on the West Coast north of Los Angeles.

Nobody at KRSC had so much as seen a TV camera yet, except for the young New Yorker Leberman hired to head up the television side. His name was Lee Schulman.

KRSC (now KAYO) at its 4th Avenue South location in Seattle. The station pioneered both FM and television broadcasting in the Puget Sound country.

1940 celebration of KRSC's new radio studios at 2939 Fourth Avenue South. Ted Bell is at center, behind the cake. Others, clockwise from left: Manager Bob Priebe, Lee Mudgett, Harold Dillon, Alex Hull, Paul Morris, George Rifkin, unidentified.

(Seattle P-I)

TV history being made. Cameramen **Jack Shawcroft** (left) and **Tom Priebe** of KRSC-TV capture high school football action for Puget Sound area's premiere telecast, Nov. 25, 1948.

The Seattle Post-Intelligencer, whose station KFC pioneered commercial radio broadcasting here in 1921, helped launch TV as well by cosponsoring the inaugural telecast.

Even the RCA chief engineer who came out to oversee installing the third-of-a-million-dollar TV plant was unsure of himself. Someone asked him how many years it takes to make a qualified television engineer. "I don't know," he replied. "There aren't any yet."

So disc jockeys were given crash courses in the mysteries of TV and then there were weeks of closed-circuit practicing before the station's grand opening broadcast took place on Thanksgiving Day, 1948.

Something like a thousand TV sets, most of them with just 8- or 10-inch screens, were tuned to Channel 5 for the inaugural telecast—a state championship high school football game at Seattle's Civic Field. Schulman's crews put in 18-hour days getting ready for the event, for which two black-and-white cameras were mounted in the stands high above the fifty-yard line, one with a wide angle lens, the second fitted with a telephoto lens for closeups.

Nine men in all wrestled with cameras, cables, sound and mixing gear, and a microwave relay transmitter mounted high up on the stadium roof.

Ted Bell, the station's veteran sportscaster, was to call the game simultaneously on TV, AM and FM radio. It was, perhaps, the first three-way simulcast in broadcasting history.

The sky was dark and threatening, the field sloppy with mud as the broadcast got underway at 1:45. Civic leaders made euphoric speeches on the field, while unpracticed engineers on the roof tweaked at the controls of the microwave transmitter, trying for a sharper picture.

(Seattle P-I)

This is how the game looked to viewers. Technical quality left a good deal to be desired but most viewers were thrilled to see discernible pictures of any kind via the newfangled medium called "television."

What they did was turn the picture negative, so that parts of the image which should have been black were sometimes white, and vice-versa.

The broadcast was scarcely a technical triumph. Halfway through the game it began to rain, and microphone cords, which had been made up from cheap war surplus cable, got wet and caused a loud hum. A transmission line failed and put the transmitter off the air for a time. But everyone thought it was

92

wonderful, and the Seattle P-I—which cosponsored the telecast—took to task those "technically minded observers, who apparently read up on the subject before attending," for finding "fault with the show when it flickered occasionally."

The game was no epic either, West Seattle and Wenatchee drawing to a muddy 6-6 tie. Some viewers got a bigger kick out of watching close-ups of the schools' "drum majorettes" at half-time.

KRSC followed the game with cartoons like "Lucky Pup" and "Devil Horse," and a film of Betty Field in a TV version of the Broadway play "Street Scene."

As the only station in town, KRSC could take its pick of shows from four networks—NBC, ABC, CBS and DuMont. Intercity cables for television were years away, though, and network programs arrived on 16-millimeter films. These "kinescope recordings" had been made by simply aiming a movie camera at a TV set screen. Definition was poor and the pictures flickered a lot.

The station used water-cooled transmitting tubes and sometimes went off the air due to hoses popping. Engineers discovered sanitary napkins made a fast temporary repair, and so kept cases and cases of Kotex pads standing by, to the invariable befuddlement of visitors.

Network programs were generally "bicycled," meaning each station shipped the film along to the next one in the chain after its own play date. Seattle was just about the end of the line. Christmas shows seemed to arrive around the same time as the first daffodils.

KRSC-TV's original, trail-blazing engineer crew. Front seat, from left: **Jack Shawcroft**, Station Manager **Bob Priebe**, and **Paul Morris**. Half-standing in rear: **Bob Ferguson**. Others, from left: **Mique Talcott**, **Ben Swisher**, Chief Engineer **George Freeman**, **Stan Carlson**, and **Clare Hanawalt**.

(Seattle Historical Society)

An early photo of **Mrs. A. Scott Bullitt**, future first lady of Seattle broadcasting, and her son **Stimson "Stim" Bullitt**, future manager of King Broadcasting. Radio was a scratchy novelty, TV a distant gleam in a few inventors' eyes when this picture was made.

A more recent portrait of the founder of King Broadcasting Co. Daughter of a Seattle lumber and real estate tycoon, **Dorothy Bullitt** entered the broadcast field with the purchase of Seattle's least listened-to radio station in 1947. From this unlikely start has evolved today's impressive empire at 320 Aurora Avenue North, which includes publishing and other ventures, besides radio and TV stations that are among the area's highest rated.

There were almost no live programs at first. A daily 10-minute newscast was filmed in New York by a press service and flown out to Seattle. Commercials were mostly "voice over"—just radio type spots read by an announcer and illustrated with slides. Everything emanated from a tiny rat-infested "studio" in an abandoned corner grocery store at 301 Galer Street on Queen Anne Hill.

When live cameras were fired up it was largely for sports events, such as the popular Monday night wrestling cards announced by Ted Bell and, later, Bill O'Mara.

O'Mara's real handle, by the way, is Rhodes. But his sponsor was the Bon Marche, which wasn't going to have its viewers reminded of that competing store down at Second and Union. So Bill changed his name.

Sponsors were wooed that way, because there were so few of them. It costs a bundle to operate a TV station—many times more than radio—and KRSC was losing not just its shirt, but its pants, vest and overcoat. P. K. Leberman was learning the truth of an old Andrew Carnegie adage: "Pioneering don't pay."

Reluctantly, he and his backers began looking for a buyer.

KOMO's Fisher family, never doubting TV would turn profitable eventually, thought of buying Channel 5 but backed out, preferring to file for a channel of their own. It was a decision they would soon regret.

So Leberman found another buyer. She was Seattle businesswoman Dorothy Stimson Bullitt, manager of two family fortunes—her father's and her late husband's—who had decided to concentrate her capital in broadcasting once the war ended. The dynamic Mrs. Bullitt *had* intended to start a new FM station in town. She'd already received a Construction Permit from the FCC, in fact, when Arch Talbot, who owned KEVR, dropped in to see her.

Talbot pleaded with her not to bring another radio station into the Puget Sound market. "There isn't enough business to go around as it is," he told her. A new station would have a mighty rugged time of it, besides making things that much harder for everyone else.

But Talbot had an idea.

"Why don't you take my station?" he asked, adding that KEVR wouldn't cost much, since "It's at the bottom of the list."

Which was true. KEVR cut a mighty feeble figure in Seattle radio. There were not many listeners, and precious few advertisers. The station operated out of a dilapidated studio in the Smith Tower—the same quarters, in fact, that the Olmsteads had fitted up for KFQX, twenty-odd years before. There were once-plush draperies still there, enveloping the studio like a tent, but looking altogether dusty and moth-eaten.

Dorothy Bullitt was quite taken with the challenge of trying to turn a losing station with no audience into a worthwhile business. She bought KEVR on May Day, 1947, and set about promoting a new image for the station.

First she needed new call letters. She wanted something pronounceable and meaningful, and of course it had to consist of four letters starting with "K." Thumbing the dictionary she ran across the word "king," which she thought would be easy to promote, and it was appropriate, Seattle being in King County and all. It was such an obvious choice, she wondered why nobody had thought of it before.

Actually, just about every broadcaster in town *had* thought of it, but for well over twenty years—as long as there had been such a thing as radio broadcasting, in fact—the government had been pronouncing that call sign "unavailable."

Unlike every other broadcaster in town, Mrs. Bullitt took the trouble to ask *why* it was unavailable. It turned out the letters had long ago been assigned to a U.S. Shipping Board freighter, the *Watertown*, as its marine radio call. So she contacted the ship's owners,

KING-TV studio about 1952. The white desk was used for commercials, besides comprising the "news set" among other things. Note simple traveling-curtain backdrop hiding rough concrete walls. The studio was a converted garage at Second Avenue West and Thomas Street in Seattle.

KING-TV's **Bill Corcoran** (under mike) chats with announcer **Bruce Calhoun** as cameraman **Tom Priebe** awaits his cue.

Calhoun emceed one of Channel 5's first remotes, when everything was still painfully new. Hired to announce the Boat Show in Seattle's Armory, Bruce got a few minutes' instruction ("This is a camera. When the red light is on, so are you.") and proceeded to ad-lib for some three hours, non-stop, without quite fainting.

negotiated a release of the call sign, and was using "KING" on station breaks by the end of June.

She also upped the power to 50,000 watts, built new studios, and began promoting the "King" motif in imaginative ways. Like getting Walt Disney to create that jaunty cartoon character, "KING Mike," who still appears in the station's newspaper ads occasionally.

Two years later, Mrs. Bullitt's King Broadcasting Co. acquired KRSC's FM and TV stations for a third of a million dollars. It was the first sale of a television station in the United States.

Meanwhile, the FCC had decided to rethink its allocations of TV frequencies, and placed a "temporary" freeze on station applications. In fact, it would be nearly five years before the freeze ended and new stations began coming on the air in the Northwest. Until then, KING had the field all to itself.

KING moved the TV studios into a sprawling garage building at Second Avenue West and Thomas Street, where Lee Schulman's ex-disc jockeys began mastering their new trade. There were some embarrassing discoveries. For instance, the first camera tubes were offshoots of World War II "snooperscopes" used for nighttime sharpshooting. They were highly

infra-red sensitive, and rather effectively saw through to the pink skins of some of the thinly-clad young ladies appearing before them.

There were no teleprompters yet. Live commercials had to be memorized. Sometimes performers forgot their lines and froze up, muttering "Take it off!" (through clenched teeth and a sweating, concrete smile) as cameramen looked on helplessly.

Murphy's Law ("whatever can go wrong, will!") was never more operative than on live TV. Lawn mowers started in rehearsal but not on the air. Or if they started, you couldn't get them to stop, and they kept buzzing all through the next part of the program.

Once Bill O'Mara was demonstrating the lubricating powers of a motor oil additive, for which an elaborate demonstration had been cobbled up consisting of weights and gears that weren't supposed to run on "Brand X" alone. You guessed it. Once on the air, the cheap oil unaccountably and repeatedly worked every bit as well as the sponsor's expensive stuff.

There were accidents, too, of both the funny and the sobering kind. Tom Dargan was directing a children's program one day when something went wrong causing him to race from the dimly lit control room into the

The irrepressible **Tom Dargan** was Channel 5's first live-audience show host. The star of "3:30 at the Norselander" is pictured here with an early wire recorder.

Stan Boreson and Art Barduhn teamed up for KING-TV's first live musical variety program, "Two B's at the Keys," in 1949. With slight format changes the show later became "Clipper Capers," then "People's Parade," "Open for Business" and finally "The Starliner." Popular under any name, the show left the air when Art took to the road with his own musical group, the Art Barduhn Trio.

studio. He tripped on a stair, burst through the studio door and rolled headlong into full view of the astonished audience. Then he uttered one shocking expletive, turned with great dignity and retreated into the control room once more.

Out at Sick's Stadium, the remote crew used to mount their cameras on the roof to cover Rainier baseball games. One time they were raising their gear on an improvised hoist when the pulley came off, sending thousands of dollars worth of cameras and equipment crashing to the street below. Fortunately, no one was standing under it.

Once a cameraman on the Stadium roof used a jackknife to splice a cable and then forgot the knife was still lying on top of the camera. During the game he tilted downward to catch some action close to the stands and the knife, still open, slid off and plummeted into the audience directly below. It landed harmlessly

between the slightly spread knees of one very startled baseball fan, after a fall of 75 feet.

Those were the days when "Uncle Miltie"—Milton Berle—was wowing nationwide audiences on Tuesday nights with his "Texaco Star Theater." Lee Schulman wanted to do something like that locally and went looking for talent.

Out at the University he caught a couple of students performing in a zany campus musical, and hired them to be the stars of KING's first-ever live music show. One was a talented pianist named Art Barduhn. The other was an accordion-playing business major from Everett, Stan Boreson.

Boreson had already traveled to several continents as a U.S.O. accompanist for singers like the Andrews Sisters and the Hoosier Hot-Shots, during the last months of the war. Now he was working his way to a degree in personnel administration by playing dance dates and helping run the Seven Cedars dance pavilion, north of Mount Vernon.*

Barduhn and Boreson blended comedy and music in their pioneering TV show, "Two Bees at the Keys," which debuted early in 1949. Not everyone appreciated their antics. Their first sponsor, a well known pie company, canceled out after the first commercial turned into an orgy of pie-throwing.

The boys snagged visiting entertainers as guests when they could. Most movie stars wouldn't be caught dead in a TV studio in those days, but gracious Gloria Swanson, whose "Sunset Boulevard" was playing all the theaters, consented to be interviewed.

Fascinated by her stories of Hollywood's early days, the crew simply ignored the clock and let the show run almost an hour too long.

Another early extravaganza on KING-TV was "March On," a weekly armed forces talent program Schulman directed himself. The show used lots of special effects, such as a smoke machine that made little wisps of "fog" to accompany moody scenes.

Once the machine went wild, gradually filling the whole studio with dense smoke. Cameramen were groping about like blind men, but it didn't really matter, because by then all the home viewers were up and fiddling with their sets, trying to tune out a solid curtain of gray "fog."

* Boreson once took a chance and signed a visiting orchestra for the pavilion, led by an as yet little known accordionist by the name of Lawrence Welk.

The original Channel 5 crew hamming it up in **KING-TV**'s studio on Second Avenue West. From left: **Stan Carlson**, **Clare Hanawalt** (on ladder), **Mique Talcott**, **Paul Sawin**, **Al Miller**, **Dave Crockett**, **Tom Priebe**, **Tom Dargan**, and **Tom Rogstad**.

Bill and **Cheri Corcoran** (on the right) were the genial emcees of "King's Kamera," an afternoon movie-and-interview show. Here they visit with **Charles Mentrin** of the Seattle Central Labor Council, and 1953 Seafair Queen **Shirley Givins**.

Wife Cheri joined Bill, a professional broadcaster, after he had been on the show for some time. She added a homey touch, and sometimes comedy relief. Once she asked some visiting entertainers: "How many are there in your quartet?"

Schulman's passion was telecasting special events. He tried to cover everything from cave-ins, fires and other disasters to Juan de Fuca channel swims. His determination was legendary, even if he wasn't always successful.

Once when Seattle was hit by a near hurricane, he had his crew throw some gear in the little remote van they called the "bread truck" and set up cameras at the Police Department's hastily established storm center. Then, in order to beam pictures back to the station, he sent technicians up to the roof of the Public Safety Building to erect a microwave transmitting antenna.

Trouble was, the antenna was some eight feet across and shaped like a pie plate. In winds gusting upwards of a hundred miles an hour, it made a fantastic kite. After nearly getting blown into Elliott Bay half a dozen times, the men convinced Schulman the job simply couldn't be done, and the program was called off.

Lee Schulman, Channel 5's pioneering program director, shaped TV in its formative years. His imaginative use of the new medium, like his early determination to cover news stories "live," is the stuff of legend.

KING-TV preparing for another "March On" extravaganza. Above, **John Daley**, **Bob Koons** and uniden-tified engineer unload gear for transfer to U.S. Navy aircraft carrier at Bremerton.

Below, **KING-TV**'s remote van, affectionately referred to as the "bread truck," is hoisted aboard. Unfortunately the microwave transmission over-water to the TV station in Seattle was unsuccessful. Channel 5 displayed a "Please Stand By" slide during most of the show.

In 1951 a totally uninhibited Southerner named Jim Lewis joined KING's afternoon lineup with the "Sheriff Tex" show. "Tex" used to sing a little, do rope tricks, show live animals. Not even the crew really knew what he would do next.

At least the livestock were predictable—they could be counted on to answer nature's call the moment someone pointed a camera their way. Preferably when it was racked to the tightest closeup lens.

Lewis took great delight in firing off a .44 pistol now and again, just to liven things up. The bullets were blank, of course, but the noise wasn't, and engineers were kept scrambling to maintain sound levels and repair blown-out microphones.

They got their revenge one day. Lewis used to hold imaginary conversations over a fake party-line telephone that was part of his set. Unknown to him, engineers wired the phone to a mike in the control room. The next time he picked up the receiver, he was greeted with an avalanche of vile observations on his appearance, his performance, his ancestry and whatnot.

Of course the audience couldn't hear any of this, but "Sheriff Tex" sure could, whether he wanted to or not, all the time he had to keep carrying on with his own routine.

Cameraman **Al Smith** dollies in for a close shot of the unpredictable "Sheriff" **Texas Jim Lewis**. Lewis is posing with a display of Christmas cards received from his young fans.

Channel 5 News Director **Charles Herring** interviews **Major John Eisenhower** at Sea-Tac Airport, about the time Eisenhower's famous father became President. In the foreground is **KING-TV** news cameraman **Ed Racine**.

Herring and Racine constituted the entire "news division" of the station when live newscasts began in September, 1951.

Point of order? In 1957 **KING-TV** sent **Charles Herring** to Washington for live coverage of the Senate Racket Committee's investigation of Dave Beck and the Teamsters Union. Morning sessions were carried live in Seattle, afternoon meetings by kinescope recording. For a local station to hire its own cross-country TV feed in those days was a stunning innovation, attracting national attention.

Pictured with Herring are Republican Senators **Joseph R. McCarthy** (left) and **Carl Mundt**. Television exposure had by this time largely discredited McCarthy, controversial figure in the anti-Red excesses of the 50's. Already ailing, he died shortly after this photo was taken.

"**Merceedes**"—and that's as much name as she ever used—was an enormously popular singer on **KING-TV** in the early 50's. She was her own accompanist, and to vary the picture a little (for how many ways are there to photograph a piano?) cameramen had a ball experimenting with novel camera angles, lap dissolves, and "supers" that looked like double exposures.

"Merceedes" sometimes added a bit of drum-like rhythm to her music by vigorously snapping the piano pedals with her foot.

TALLULAH

NO MO

Your friend
Stan Boreson

Stan Boreson and friends pose in the set of "King's Clubhouse," **KING-TV**'s enormously popular program for the after-school crowd.

"No Mo Shun," Boreson's lethargic bassett hound, was a regular on the show—and made a big hit by never doing anything at all. Actually there were two different No Mo's. Boreson quickly substituted a look-alike after the first pet was killed by a car.

Boreson's "Password" theme song was written for him by organist Elliott Brown:

"Zero dachus, Mucho Crackus
  Hallaballooza Bub
That's the secret password that we
  Use down at the club, and
Zero dachus, Mucho Crackus
  Hallaballooza fan
Means now you are a member of
  King's T.V. club with Stan."

Surely the most beloved of KING's programs for smaller children was "Wunda Wunda." Ruth Prins, who played the story-telling clown, had been appearing as the "Story Lady" on Gloria Chandler's weekly show for the small fry called "Telaventure Tales." In 1953 she proposed a daily two-hour offering for preteens and Lee Schulman bought the idea.

"Wunda Wunda" started in October of that year, later dropping back to a single hour daily. ("Sometimes you just get tired," Ruth explained.) By the time the series ended in 1972 it had won a Peabody award, and just about every other TV award there is, too.

Ruth recruited a veteran vaudeville organist, Elliott Brown, to play background music on the show. He also wrote her theme song: *Wunda Wunda is my name, Boys and girls, I'm glad you came....*

Brown had played in silent movie theaters in Chicago, where he had a nodding acquaintance with the celebrated gangster, Al Capone. On "Wunda Wunda" he surrounded himself with organ, piano, celeste, xylophone, drums and anything else he could think of, and seemed to play them all simultaneously, meanwhile puffing away furiously on the big, smelly cigars he adored.

Wunda Wunda usually opened her show by putting her head out of the Wunda House window and greeting an animal friend. One day she looked up toward the sky calling "Hello, Bluebird, where are you?" Just then she felt a contact lens slipping. Quickly raising a finger to rub one eye and still gazing upward she went right on, "Oh! *There* you are!"

Ruth's story-telling was often accompanied by ingenious video effects, dreamed up by an inspired crew and involving rear screen projectors, or miniature sets,

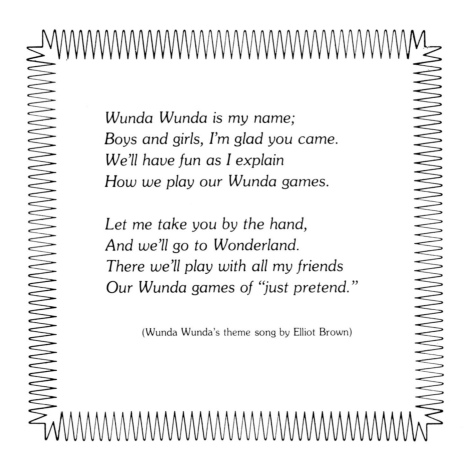

Wunda Wunda is my name;
Boys and girls, I'm glad you came.
We'll have fun as I explain
How we play our Wunda games.

Let me take you by the hand,
And we'll go to Wonderland.
There we'll play with all my friends
Our Wunda games of "just pretend."

(Wunda Wunda's theme song by Elliot Brown)

→

Ruth Prins began her long career on TV as the Story Lady on "Telaventure Tales" over **KING-TV**. The show started in 1950, to be followed by the award-winning "Wunda Wunda" program in October, 1953. Here with Ruth is the program's creator, **Gloria Chandler**.

Ruth Prins pets "Little Tyke," supposedly tame lion borrowed for the Wunda Wunda show. Note rear-screen projected jungle background scene. "Little Tyke" does not seem to be enjoying the experience.

or painted backgrounds that moved. The permanent set was the Wunda House front surrounded by cuddly, stuffed animals.

Bored night crewmen, equally inspired, used to pass their time contorting the animals' limbs into bizarre—usually obscene—configurations for the amusement of the next day's crew, which of course had to correct these shocking depravities before air time.

Sometimes live animals were used on the program. When Ruth did the story "Elephant Child" her director, Bill Stevens, brought a charming baby elephant from Woodland Park onto the set. The show was a captivating success. So when Ruth later planned to read a lion story, Bill negotiated with a private owner for the appearance of a supposedly tame feline.

The lion sat obligingly by Ruth's side during the first

Moments later "Tyke" attacked Ruth's arm, held it between clenched teeth while Wunda Wunda finished telling her story. Now it's Ruth's turn to wish she were somewhere else.

part of the tale, then took a dislike to Wunda Wunda's gesturing arm and seized it purposefully between powerful jaws.

Ruth kept on reading. The lion, glaring, kept holding her arm. She could feel the clown costume tearing, the bruises rising, the skin ready to break.

At length the lion released its grip and began prowling the studio. Cameramen locked their "brown-ies" in place and climbed ladders. Floor directors scattered. Elliott Brown, busy at the organ, felt something nuzzling his behind and—as he put it—"suddenly found the lost chord."

But they all survived the show, which was live, of course, and no blood was spilled either. Ruth has a kinescope recording of the whole thing which she thinks is pretty funny—now.

Unplanned drama on the "Wunda Wunda" show. At left, police escort a manacled burglary suspect through the set during an evening's taping session. He was discovered prowling an adjacent furniture store and brought out a fire door leading to the KING-TV studio. At right, Wunda Wunda reacts to the interruption. Director Al Smith kept the tape rolling and broadcast it moments later on the 10 o'clock news.

Bea Donovan, **KING-TV**'s longtime home economist, demonstrates the proper way to de-wing a Christmas turkey on her pioneering show for homemakers, "King's Queen."

Above: Co-hosts **Casey Gregarson** and **Mike Rhodes** on **KING-TV**'s long-running daytime feature program, "Telescope." Lower photo: a gaggle of Channel 5 personalities talking it up on a later version of the show. From left, **Irene Malbin**, **Howard Hall**, **Bea Donovan**, and **Elizabeth Leonard**. Note how set designers' progressive abstractions have replaced the plain gray backdrops of TV's earlier days. (See page 95.)

CHAPTER EIGHT

"The Naked Truth"

It is a fascinating thing to consider the love-hate relationship that has always existed between broadcasting and the newspapers. As late as 1977 Eric Sevareid, the dean of network commentators, was remarking on a "restrained animosity" still subsisting between the two media.

And yet newspapers themselves were enthusiastic founders of many pioneer broadcasting stations. This was certainly true in the Puget Sound country, where the Post-Intelligencer's KFC initiated commercial radio (as opposed to amateur experimenting) back in 1921. Tacoma's daily paper, the Ledger, got its broadcasting license the same day as the P-I, though it was some months before its station, KGB, got into operation. And the Bellingham Herald took to the air shortly thereafter—just as newspapers all across the land were doing.

Harry Higgins, visionary managing editor of the Tacoma paper, was especially enthusiastic. He felt that any device a man could use to talk to the Ledger's subscribers would wind up competing with the paper one day. "We should get IN, now!" he said, and he did. It was he who arranged with Mullins Electric Co. and the flamboyant Alvin Stenso to put KGB on the air for the paper.

But his views were not shared by fellow executives at the Ledger. Higgins passed away suddenly, early in 1923, and the radio station went into a decline. One day it simply signed off the air and never came back on again.

Much the same thing was happening with other newspaper-owned radio stations. Even the Seattle P-I decided, in the summer of 1924, to close down its historic three-year-old station. There was a tearful last broadcast, for which Mac Spurling's six-piece band and a mouth organist named Syd Brockman mounted the iron stairs to the shack on the P-I roof one last time.

The broadcast was supposed to end at midnight. But firemen listening in on crystal sets at a nearby fire hall sent up coffee and sandwiches, so Spurling and Brockman carried on for an extra two hours.

Carl Haymond, the station's pioneer announcer-engineer, had meanwhile been hired away to run Rhodes Department Store's KFOA. Under his guiding hand the station was to break new ground as Puget Sound's most innovative voice. (More on this in Chapter 10.)

Haymond was tall, sturdy, handsome as a movie star. By 1925, this ex-Cornell football player who neither smoke nor drank was already a triple-threat broadcaster. Whether performing, engineering or managing, he knew radio stations from the microphone right up to the antenna. He was full of ideas, too, but the Rhodes company didn't always go for them. So he figured he'd just have to get a station of his own.

There were half a dozen outfits on the air in Seattle by this time, and three or four more due to start up. But ever since the demise of KGB, only one station remained in Tacoma. And it didn't amount to much.

KMO in Tacoma had started as 7XV, a ham rig in Howard Reichert's house at North 9th and L Streets. It was relicensed under the new call letters to Love Electric Company in 1922. Haymond offered to buy the call sign and that blue piece of government paper. Meanwhile he was looking at a transmitter for sale down in Portland.

Haymond needed 3,000 bucks to swing the deal. All he had was the equity on his house; that netted him two thousand. Then one day Al Hubbard, Olmstead's engineer, offered him $1000 to go up to Ketchikan and install a station there for an associate of his. Haymond said OK, and caught the next boat.

The Ketchikan station's call was KGBU. It turned out to be our old friend the Tacoma Ledger station, with a fourth letter added to the call sign, and the ebullient Alvin Stenso again in charge of the programming side.

Inaugural show from Winthrop Hotel radio studios of **KMO**, Tacoma, August 26, 1926. Broadcasting pioneer **Carl Haymond** (right) poses with **Bill Winder** (at piano) and his orchestra.

Haymond arrived in Alaska to find a big part of his job was to rebuild a lot of ancient equipment to meet current technical standards. And the somewhat puritanical Carl Haymond was in for another surprise. Hubbard's "hotel" turned out to be one of Ketchikan's more infamous brothels.

There were certain parts, tools, etc. Haymond found he needed for the job but all his urgent messages to Hubbard went unheeded. Finally in desperation he had his wife run Hubbard down in person.

She found him all right—in jail!

Hubbard was awaiting trial for his part in the alleged liquor conspiracy. (He confided, though, that in fact he was a government agent—planted to keep tabs on Olmstead. And that may well be. Nobody has ever been able to say for sure which side Hubbard was really on.)

Haymond never did get paid for his work in the Ketchikan bagnio, though Hubbard sent him his daily prisoner's allowance of cigarette money which helped with the expenses incurred. Nor would anybody loan him the funds to buy KMO. ("Radio?" asked the bankers; "What's that?") But in the end someone turned up to go partners with him, and he was able to buy the station in 1926.

Then he found out the fellow he bought it from didn't actually own KMO!

Fortunately the real owner was tender-hearted and agreed to sell on the same terms, rather than see the culprit jailed over Haymond's complaint. All the legal tangles weren't unsnarled until just minutes before the gala inaugural broadcast hit the air that summer.

And what a broadcast! It originated from KMO's rooftop studios over Tacoma's swank Winthrop Hotel, and featured everything from Bill Winder's hotel orchestra to the 10th Field Artillery Band from Fort Lewis.

KMO turned out to be a family business. Haymond's wife, Margaret, became a radio performer in her own right, using the radio name "Jane Morse." She sang and played the piano. She hosted a popular children's program. She handled the station's bookkeeping and secretarial work. And if her husband had to go out of town on business she was the boss until he got back.

113

The look of old-time radio. This natty, unidentified impresario is broadcasting by "remote control" from somewhere around Tacoma, about 1930. This may be one of those dance marathon broadcasts that were all the rage. Note that **KMO** was still using "double-button" carbon microphones.

Before the days of scintillating chroma-keyed animated satellite photographs and spinning, sliding, flashing multi-hued display boards, weather reporting was done with chalk and a blackboard map. Here **Bob Gleason** of **KTNT-TV**, Tacoma, explains why it rained again today.

called it the American Meatcutters Association, and insisted M.D. stands for "more dough." He also claimed appendicitis operations are unnecessary and that vaccinations cause syphilis.

Convicted, finally, of practicing medicine without a license, Baker (whose radio support in the Midwest helped put his friend and fellow Iowan Herbert Hoover in the White House) was sentenced to one day in jail.

But the Federal Radio Commission came down harder. Baker's broadcasting license was revoked—an almost totally unique case in tolerant America of license recision because of program content.

In 1947 there probably weren't over a few thousand FM sets in the whole Puget Sound country, but the new KTNT had a captive audience. The Trib put receivers in all the city buses, thus guaranteeing plenty of ears for its commercial messages.

KTNT added an AM station in 1948, and when TV

applications were unfrozen in 1952, filed for one of two channels allocated to Tacoma. The permit to go on channel 11 was granted later in the year.

KTNT's engineers raced to get on the air as quickly as possible. The transmitter and antenna were finished first, and for some weeks the station telecast an Indian head test pattern accompanied by a tedious audio tone. Meanwhile viewers all over the Northwest, who had been getting along fine with a single-channel antenna pointed to Seattle, were adding shorter "Tacon" antennas for the new channel and aiming them at Tacoma.

Then on the evening of March 1, engineers cut away from the test pattern to an almost identical image: station manager Len Higgins, in profile, resplendently decked out in a feathered war bonnet like the test pattern Redskin. Higgins then turned slowly to the camera, removed the gaudy headdress with a sly grin, and welcomed viewers to the Northwest's second TV station.

125

There were three more television signals to come alive in that memorable year: Carl Haymond's KMO-TV on channel 13; KVOS-TV in Bellingham; and finally in December, Fisher's Blend Station's KOMO-TV on channel 4.

KOMO executives had fairly gnashed their teeth down to the gums all this while. They had applied for TV way back in 1948, but construction had been held up, first by a challenge to their application; next by the FCC "freeze"; and then by endless red tape. Meanwhile they arranged with the University to conduct training classes for the station's personnel, and put on weeks of closed circuit practice programs, using the windows of department stores as studios.

From the point of view of money, television is an entirely different kettle of trout than radio. TV equipment is enormously expensive. The daily operational costs are staggering, particularly if a station has to produce all of its programs. And even the best local

Station owner **Carl Haymond** (left) and General Manager **Jerry Geehan** on the tube. Inaugural telecast of **KMO-TV**, Tacoma, Aug. 2, 1953.

Orville Dennis and **Jack Shepard** in the control room of **KMO-TV**, Tacoma, about 1953. Note the two revolving slide drums, center, and larger movie projectors on each side. Images from all these sources were "multiplexed" by means of movable mirrors into a single film-chain camera.

Francis Brott, KOMO's longtime chief engineer, poses with the station's first TV camera in 1953. At right are KOMO executives **Stan Bennett** and **Willard "Bill" Warren**.

Brott had conducted the Puget Sound area's first-ever experimental television broadcasts, back in 1929. He was also one of the area's first radio broadcasters, having announced and played cylinder recordings over his amateur station **7AD** as early as June, 1921.

Live TV color came to the Puget Sound country Feb. 1, 1956. There were hardly any color sets in homes as yet. But **KOMO-TV** officials, having failed (by five years!) to be first on the air with black-and-white, were determined to lead the way with color.

Promotion for the inaugural colorcast included appearances by model **Carol Price** (as "Miss Colorvision") and Washington State Governor **Arthur B. Langlie**.

shows can scarcely compete with the networks' slick productions. In the fifties, it seemed doubtful a station could survive at all, except as a net outlet.

So both KTNT and KMO were gambling. They gambled that by getting on the air fast, before the Seattle channels, they could sign those precious contracts with CBS and NBC, respectively. And that's just the way it worked out.

No sooner did KOMO come on the air, though, than NBC exercised some fine print in their contract and switched to the Fisher station.

So, unfortunately for KMO, did most of the viewers.

Now Carl Haymond and "Lucky Channel 13" (as the station was promoting itself) were in big trouble. Whole regiments of advertisers waited just until the Christmas rush ended to send in their cancellations. By New Year's Day the red ink was flowing and to Haymond, it might have been his own life's blood draining away. Everything he had ever worked for was like to go down the tube.

So he called in the high-powered salesmen, the production people and the talent he had hired from New York and Hollywood, and fired them. He moved his tiny studio from behind the Rialto Theater downtown, to even tinier quarters at the transmitter plant in Tacoma's north end. Pioneering again, he figured out a way for one man to run the whole operation— announcing, film handling, sound, cameras—everything.

But nothing worked. Finally he hung out a for-sale sign and Channel 13 changed hands the next year. Then it changed hands again, and again, and yet again. In time, with FCC permission, it became KCPQ, an educational station operated by the Clover Park school system. And now, under yet *another* set of owners, it has recently reverted back to *commercial* status again—apparently the first and only station in the country ever to make such a switch.

Seattle's folk-singing humorist **Ivar Haglund** regales **Don McCune**, emcee of the **KOMO-TV** "Captain Puget" and "Exploration Northwest" series, with his Puget Sound version of "The Twelve Days of Christmas." The Haglund parody calls for a seagull in a fir tree, followed by two dozen oysters, three cracked crabs, four silver salmon, five red snappers, six sacks of clams, seven shiny smelt, etc. etc.

Adman **Jerry Hoeck** (left) with NBC's **Bill Guyman** and Pacific National Advertising Agency president **Trevor Evans** in 1956. Guyman's ''Morning Report'' was co-sponsored by the Seattle-based Bardahl and Fisher Flour companies.

KOMO-TV's ''Miss Colorvision'' poses with home economist **Katherine Wise** (whose real name is **Ruth Fratt**) and **Dick Keplinger**, stars of ''Cookbook Quiz.'' The program combined elements of the recipe shows that were standard daytime fare on early TV, and the game shows that were destined to replace them.

(CBS)

''I Love Lucy,'' seen Monday nights on Channel 11 in the 50's was one of TV's most popular programs ever. Unlike most series then it was produced on film, not live. So today, through reruns, **Lucy** and **Desi** go on—and on—and on.

KING-TV's **Al Wallace** relaxes on the set of ''How Come?'' Al's TV career began in the announce booth of Channel 11, Tacoma, in the early 50's. He joined King Broadcasting as a newsman after a few years, and is known these days for his reporting of feature stories.

Now one last channel allocation in Seattle was up for grabs. KIRO, KXA, KVI and just about everybody else was trying frantically to get it. The hearings, filings, counterfilings and appeals dragged on and on. Meanwhile Tacoma's KTNT-TV, with all the top-rated CBS programs—Ed Sullivan, "Playhouse 90," Jackie Gleason, "Gunsmoke," the Doug Edwards news—was riding high up at the top of the rating charts, and so selling commercials and practically printing money.

And there was a lot of local programming. The obligatory mid-morning cooking, home-making, and interview show, for instance, emceed by Bob Gleason and Connie Page. We were all still learning our craft, then. Sometimes, things actually went according to plan.

Neither host actually cooked on the program. The guests were supposed to do that. But one day when Betty ("The Egg and I") McDonald was supposed to whip up something scrumptious, her ferry from Vashon Island ran aground and left her stranded at the dock. Bob and Connie wound up with an embarrassed hour to fill. Nothing in the 'fridge but hen's fruit, either.

So the staff cooked eggs.

For an hour, yet.

At KTNT we really believed in TV as a tool for the general good. Our obligatory afternoon children's program was called "Dandy Time" and featured "Dandy Din," who was Din Fuhrmeister. Din was a patient, soft-spoken ex-bomber pilot who was genuinely fond of children. A group of them came to the station every day, and Din answered their questions, let them show some favorite toy, and then taught them something about crafts, or art, or Indian lore, or whatever.

But somehow the show didn't catch on. The kids wanted more action. And so a program was devised using old Roy Rogers and Gene Autry films. These were wholesome Western adventures in which the heroes always won out through clean living and right thinking.

In the intermissions, live audiences of kids were to be taught about arts and crafts or Indian lore.

This format didn't do too well either, so the moral Western movies were replaced by Bugs Bunny cartoons, and the arts and crafts were dropped in favor of occasional comedy appearances by an irreverent puppet known as "Crazy Donkey."

This version of the show was a great success. When it left the air, finally, a few years ago, it was one of the longest-running kids' programs in the country.

The show used a model train setup as an identifying gimmick and the emcee was supposed to be a young

Dinwiddie Fuhrmeister as "Dandy Din" on the children's show "Dandy Time." **KTNT-TV**, Tacoma, in 1954.

Bill McLain togged out as "Brakeman Bill" with "Crazy Donkey"— played by **Warren Reed**—perched on his shoulder. **KTNT-TV**, about 1957.

Warren Reed, the unseen articulator of Brakeman Bill's upstart puppet, "Crazy Donkey." He was also Channel 11's unconventional late-show host, appearing in outrageous costumes and sets to spoof the station's old movies between reels.

Channel 11's **Bill McLain** cuts up on the station's front stoop, while waiting for the day's "Brakeman Bill" show to air. With him is a bemused **Bob Gleason**, who directed the program.

fellow called "Engineer Walt." Just before the first episode went on the air "Walt" contracted polio and a KTNT cameraman named Bill McLain was drafted, almost at the last moment, to fill in as "Brakeman Bill."

"Walt" emerged from the hospital after a few weeks and took over the show for a while, with costume overalls hiding leg and back braces, and crutches always waiting just out of camera range. But live TV is rugged work in the best of cases, and it was a great relief to all concerned when McLain later returned as the show's permanent host.

Bill has made a fine career for himself and "Walt," his health restored, has gone happily on to other pursuits in and out of broadcasting, such as writing the book you are now reading.

The author as "Engineer Walt," on **KTNT-TV** Channel 11 in 1955. The series switched formats and emcees the following year, with former cameraman Bill McLain starring as "Brakeman Bill."

CHAPTER NINE

"The Musical Station"

When I was a young squirt back in the thirties our family lived for a time at Deep Lake, two whoops and a holler up a dirt road leading north from Tenino. The Depression was very much on and about the only signal we could get clearly with our cheap table-top Philco was KGY, a little record station in Olympia.

There were two remarkable things about KGY. They were forever advertising a sale of cut glass dishes on the local department store's third floor. And all the announcers sounded exactly alike.

We never did learn why Mottman's overstocked all those pickle dishes, but years afterward I got to know and work with Earl Thoms, who actually was KGY's one and only announcer back in those hungry years.

Talk about a full-time job! Earl came in at sign-on each morning and stayed until sign-off at night, day in and day out, with no provision at all for days off, vacations or sick leave. He read all the commercials and played all the records. In "spare" moments he repaired any equipment that broke down, answered the telephone, rewrote ads and kept the floor swept.

If the transmitter needed major work, he had to stay even later at night and get that done too.

Earl's wife would bring him meals from home twice a day, on the city bus, cradling hot dishes in a covered sauce pan on her lap, or in Mason jars wrapped in newspaper. They would visit briefly while Earl wolfed down these repasts between announcements, and they probably reflected on how fortunate he was to be working. That's how it was in the thirties.

Not all stations were like KGY, of course. Earl Thoms got paid a fair wage in real cash. Some operations couldn't afford that and handed out merchandise collected from advertisers in return for commercial time.

KGY's news department was the fellow who ran the coffee shop downstairs. He'd come up to the studio and read news he'd scrounged somewhere—probably out of the daily paper—in return for plugging the coffee shop.

There were two other people working at KGY. Ricky Bras, the manager, spent most of his time drumming up business around town. And there was a girl receptionist who kept the accounts, scheduled commercials and wrote up the "spots" that Bras phoned in.

Ricky Bras was actually a musician—a fine pianist and singer. The receptionist-bookkeeper-continuity writer had a nice voice, too, and Earl himself could carry a decent tune when called on. The three of them put on a live show early each morning. Songs and patter. Time and weather reports. Bad jokes and pickle dish ads. That was small-time radio in the Depression.

Earl Thoms, an unflappable youth with black, black hair and the debonair shadow of a mustache, had been bitten by the radio bug in the late twenties. Between stints as a shipboard wireless operator he had worked briefly for a couple of small record stations in Seattle. His ambition was to get on with KOL, the big CBS-Don Lee outlet owned by Archie Taft. It happens that Taft was also the owner of KGY.

So Earl was sent to work in Olympia with the promise of a job at KOL, eventually, if he "behaved himself."

Taft made good his promise after three years or so. Earl moved to KOL about the time the station lost CBS, and remained there until the war broke out. Still doubling and tripling in brass, he was variously sound effects man, studio engineer, transmitter operator, and announcer.

133

Announce booth and record playing equipment at **KXA**, around 1931.

The two Seattle stations Earl had worked for earlier, around 1930, were KFQW and KXA. The former was a short-lived station run by Vincent Kraft's kid brother, Edwin. A UW graduate engineer and one-time shipmate of Nick Foster, Ed was not an easy man to work for. One Federal Radio Commission file describes him as "hopelessly insolvent and very bull-headed." The station's license was finally yanked in 1931 because Kraft couldn't keep KFQW on the right frequency.

KFQW was located in half of a tiny block-like structure on the roof of the Continental Hotel at 315 Seneca Street. Earl recalls the radio station side was "about the size of a kitchenette." The other half contained motors and relays for the hotel's elevators, which KFQW's listeners could generally hear banging and slamming away in the background.

The station had an assigned power of 200 watts, which Kraft derived from a bank of storage batteries. The actual output power dropped steadily all day as the batteries got weaker and weaker.

KXA was the station Ed's big brother Vincent bought from Roy Olmstead back in 1926. He had the call sign changed late the following year, rebuilt the transmitter and moved the station into the Bigelow Building at Fourth and Pike.

There were two rather cramped studios and a control room on the second floor. A wire from the transmitter ran out the window and up to the roof, where two windmill towers supported a "flattop" antenna. The station's soundproofing was perfunctory, so that occasionally you could hear yowls from the credit dentistry offices just down the hall.

In 1935, Roland Meggee became manager of KXA. He later bought out Kraft's interest to become owner of the station.

Meggee moved the transmitter down to the Alexander Steamship terminal—better known after the war started as the Port of Embarkation—and repeated KVI's stunt by erecting the station's brand-new slant-fed antenna tower at the end of a long pier, on a foundation rising straight out of the salt chuck. He

KXA transmitter room, Bigelow Building, in the early 30's.

also got the frequency changed from 570 to 770 kilocycles, practically a clear channel.* These changes improved the station's signal tremendously. Reception reports began coming in from as far away as Australia.

KXA promoted itself as "The Musical Station" and tried to program a little something for everyone. Like record stations everywhere just then, it broke the day into discrete quarter and half-hour program periods, each with its own theme song, format, sponsor, and music style. Fifteen minutes of songs by Harry Owens' Royal Hawaiians might be followed by a quarter hour of Bing Crosby records, then a half hour of "cowboy" tunes (as country-Western music was loosely called in that era). And so on and on, all day long.

The mid-morning program of Hawaiian music, by the way, was sponsored by Harry Druxman, who advertised as the Northwest's "Square Deal Jeweler." KXA announcer Jack Latham made one of the area's

classic bloopers the day his tongue slipped and he redubbed Druxman the "Square Jew Dealer."

Meanwhile, New York's WNEW was experimenting with a new approach to record programming. "Disc Jockeys" like Martin Block and Stan Shaw were on the air for hours at a stretch, wowing their audiences with their personality and chatter. Shaw's immensely popular, late-night "Milkman's Matinee" show even invited listeners to wire record requests and dedications to him. The Western Union printer was right in the studio, where Stan would "up and read" telegrams on the air as they came in.

Jack Latham, who was KXA's program director, decided to try the same stunt in Seattle. Charlie Barnette's recording of "Stay-Up Stan, the All Night Record Man" provided him with both the title and theme song. Now, Latham needed an announcer.

The man he picked was a young, soft-spoken but

* WJZ (now WABC) in New York retained first claim to the frequency. To this day KXA must sign off the air between local sunset and about 10 p.m., to avoid skywave interference with the big eastern station.

135

pleasingly glib University student named Jim Neidigh, whose father was a dentist in the Seattle offices of "Painless Parker."

Neidigh had been on radio before. He'd worked briefly for KFIO, Spokane, without any pay, just to gain experience.

"Stay-Up Stan" aired on KXA from midnight to 3 a.m. and was an immediate sensation. Neidigh plugged hard for requests and dedications, and there was no messing around with Western Union telegrams. "Fling a ring to SEneca 1000" was his slogan, and all night the phone lines were jammed with callers asking to play "Stardust" for Jane, and Bill, and that cute red-head in the next office.

KXA was a "combo station," that is, its announcers were ordinarily required to hold FCC licenses and combine technical duties with air work. Neidigh was an exception to this rule, so Latham needed an engineer to work the night shift with him. About that time a brash, smooth-talking fellow blew into town from somewhere in Alaska, flashed his FCC "ticket"

"Fling a ring—to SEneca 1000!" **Jim Neidigh**, Seattle's original "Stay Up Stan," was an enormously popular all-night record request emcee on **KXA** beginning in 1939. He was the first of the big personality DJ's on Puget Sound radio.

Neidigh is pictured here at **KRSC** (later **KAYO**) where he moved in 1948, just in time to help pioneer TV on Channel 5.

John H. Dubuque, chief engineer and popular announcer at **KXA**, Seattle in 1947. He's shown here at the control board of KXA's Bigelow Building studio, reading a "spot" announcement and preparing simultaneously to cue up a sound effect record on the near turntable.

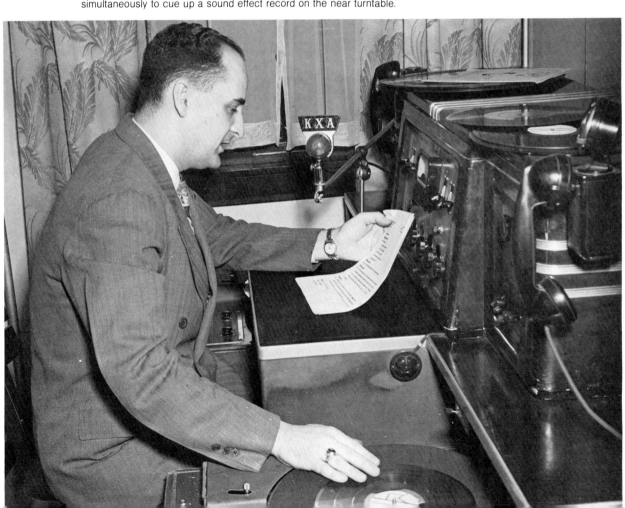

and asked for a job. His name was Jan King.

King worked the technical side of the night shift for a while, filling out his hours with some daytime announcing. Then Latham decided to try an afternoon version of Neidigh's request show, and King became its emcee.

The program was "The Spook Club." It came on at 4 o'clock and was aimed squarely at teenagers just getting home from school.

And the youngsters went wild. You just weren't "in" if you didn't listen every day. King discouraged telephone requests, but every mail delivery brought bags of letters, and when a really popular platter like Jimmy Dorsey's "Green Eyes" was played, it could take ten minutes to read all the dedications.

Jimmie Lunceford, the famous band leader, came through town and King jollied him into recording a theme song for the program. It was called "Hi, Spook."

There were special appearances and even remote broadcasts from places like Seattle's Roller Rink. King even formed a band of his own and would rent the big Trianon Ballroom to hold dances for Spook Club members. It was really a big deal if you belonged to that generation.

But Jan King was a rolling stone and one day he simply packed up and left town to seek some new adventure elsewhere. The "Spook Club" passed quickly into legend. It was replaced by "The Smartest Music on Record," a decidedly less frantic but also quite popular show featuring big-band records. The disc jockey was John Dubuque, who took all the music magazines and kept listeners abreast of where the bands were playing and what all the singers and musicians were doing.

Dubuque was also the station's long-suffering chief engineer. His tribulations began shortly after America went to war at the end of 1941.

First the Army moved into the steamship terminal, where KXA's tower rose out of the salt water, and began dredging a channel nearby for its big transport ships. One day John looked up and noticed the tower was starting to lean a little bit. The next day it was leaning even more. And the more the Army dredged the channel, the more KXA's tower resembled the one over in Pisa.

Obviously the tower had to come down, and quickly, before it fell. None of the local riggers would risk working on the structure, but John found some specialists somewhere who came in and managed to disassemble it in the nick of time.

Meanwhile he ran a temporary wire antenna right out of the transmitter, through a window and over to a nearby City Light pole.

This expedient worked fairly well, except that one day an announcer named Ken Meyer forgot it was there, climbed up on a stool to reach for something, and drew a spark that burned off all his hair. Zapp! Instant Kojack.

KIRO had just moved out of KFOA's old penthouse transmitter shack on top of the Rhodes store, having built its big, new plant over on Vashon Island. So KXA arranged to take over the rooftop of the department store. By this time, military service and the defense industry were siphoning off all the able-bodied young men and John Dubuque wound up practically moving the station up to Rhodes by himself.

Announcers were leaving right and left for the war. To fill the gap, stations like KXA began hiring inexperienced teen-agers right out of high school. The

Following Pearl Harbor many radio stations began losing their best men to the war effort. Artist Sid Hix drew this cartoon, bewailing the plight of station executives, for Broadcasting Magazine's June, 1942 issue.

Drawn for BROADCASTING by Sid Hix

"I Understand You're Interested In Hiring An Announcer Who's Draft Exempt?"

137

The author as a very young announcer, **KXA**, 1943.

author of this book, for example. It became an industry joke: read a spot, put on a record, and resume playing some kid game.

We were a callow lot, and not yet all that technically minded. One day Warren Brown, all of sixteen years old, was on duty when the old water-cooled transmitter sprang a leak. Escaping moisture hit the high voltage, causing sparks like Roman candles to shoot out the front to the accompaniment of ominous sizzling noises and a great deal of smoke. Warren shot out of his seat like a bullet and watched from behind a door until finally a fuse blew, ending the fireworks.

It was a weird transmitter, anyway, with a mind and will of its own. Especially at sign-on time each morning. You pushed a little black button to warm up the tube filaments, waited a bit and pushed a big green one marked "start." Nothing happened, as a rule. So then you turned up a gigantic rheostat that increased the voltage as high as you dared, while jabbing at the recalcitrant button; and if the transmitter still didn't take off, there was a big "X" painted on the back panel where you were supposed to give it a sound rap.

This was usually administered in the form of a swift kick, and always with great personal satisfaction, if not much technical effect.

The last resort was to tug on a string that hung from the beast's innards, with a bottle opener tied on the end. That usually did the trick, but if it didn't, there was nothing for it but to telephone John Dubuque at home. Like as not he would have been up all night doing maintenance, but he would come along in a few minutes, sleepy-eyed and mumbling something about children and the Foreign Legion.

There were lots of shortages during the war. KXA decided to do a daily program from Bremerton, where business was booming at the Navy Yard. There was no

By September the situation had worsened to where this follow-up cartoon by Hix scarcely exaggerated what could actually be seen in control rooms across the land.

Drawn for BROADCASTING by Sid Hix

"Goody, Goody, a Network Show . . . Now I Can Get Back to My War for a Half-hour!"

138

studio space to be had, so arrangements were made to use the foyer of the women's lavatory at the Elks Club. After the first few programs were marred by embarrassing background noises, the station made up a neat little sign:

Please Do Not Flush Toilet While Radio Station Is On.

The war ended eventually. One by one the old-timers came back to their microphones. Jim Neidigh resumed his role as "Stay-Up Stan" just hours after he climbed out of an Army uniform. Earl Thoms, back from the South Pacific, joined the crew at KXA. So did Earl Reilly and Len Beardsley.

Beardsley has one of the smoothest voices ever to come out of Seattle. You can hear him these days on nighttime ABC-TV shows coming from Hollywood. His breath control is fantastic. Once at KXA, on a dare, he did an entire newscast standing on his head and never even gulped.

Reilly was an even greater cut-up. On sunny days he used to take an extension mike out onto the roof of Rhodes, and lie on a cot sunning himself and announcing while some mike-struck teen-ager he'd befriended ran the control board inside.

Len Beardsley's was one of the top announcing voices to come out of Seattle in the 40's. Len went to ABC in Los Angeles in 1951 and is that network's West Coast television voice these days.

Earl Thoms at the operating console of **KXA**, atop Seattle's Rhodes Department Store in May, 1948.

Reilly was "Spike Hogan," emcee of a popular cowboy music program called the "Friendly Trail." His announcements, done in a hokey hillbilly accent, were the ultimate spoof of all Western programs.

Earl also promoted a series of Friendly Trail dances, and almost got into trouble one time when he hired a small plane to drop silver-painted paper plates over Seattle and Bremerton as an advertising stunt. That's when the flying saucer phenomenon was quite new and somewhat alarming. Military radar picked up the "saucers" all over Puget Sound and there was no end of commotion for a while.

It seemed a lot of the station's announcers were promoting themselves extra income one way or another. One enterprising KXA personality used to run a string of juke boxes in the waiting rooms of Seattle's First Avenue brothels.

The "Friendly Trail" gang on **KXA**. At top is **Earl Reilly** as "Spike Hogan." At the bottom, from left, are **Al Bowles** as "Pink Eye," **Len Beardsley** as "Clem," **John** "Shorta" **Dubuque**, and **Bob McCoy** as "Slim."

Earl Reilly (left) interviewing **Tennessee Ernie Ford** on the "Friendly Trail" program about 1946. The show originated from **KXA**'s transmitting loft atop the Rhodes store in Seattle. (Note transmitter and early tape gear in background.)

To Ford's delight, Reilly—as "Spike Hogan," the irrepressible hillbilly—kept calling him "Tennis Shoe Ernie."

KXA Disc Jockey **Bill Apple**. Apple was "Stay Up Stan," emcee of the popular nighttime request program during World War 2 years.

Radio began to change right after the war. For one thing, a lot of new stations were coming on the air, some of them in towns once considered too small to support a station. One of the first of these was Leo Beckley's KBRC in Mount Vernon. (The last three letters are for "**B**eckley **R**adio **C**ompany.")

We always addressed Leo as "Colonel." He'd just been separated with that rank from the Army, where he'd served in the cavalry. (Yes, cavalry. He loved horses passionately, and always kept a few pastured at the back door of the station.)

Leo still projected a kind of dour military gruffness, but inside, his heart, lungs and liver were 24-karat. He'd been a newspaperman up until the war, and hadn't so much as seen the inside of a radio station before. Everybody figured he'd go broke within the year; but he didn't.

The pay was less than princely at first. One newly-wed announcer shared a rented farmhouse attic with his bride and a large family of mice, and got to work each day on a borrowed bicycle. But there was a rare spirit of fun and country camaraderie about KBRC too, that you couldn't measure in dollars.

A lot of young people broke into broadcasting there, and after gaining a few months' experience, moved on to the larger stations in Seattle and Tacoma.

250-watt radio tower of **KRKO**, Wetmore and Wall Streets, Everett, in the 40's. The station was originally **KFBL**, licensed to Otto and Bob Leese, Everett auto repairmen. Their chief announcer was Clarence "Doc" Miller, the local chiropractor. KFBL powered its transmitter with a bank of car batteries which, its brochure proudly noted, produced a voltage "more than three times sufficient for an electric chair."

"KRSC's Program Department takes you now to the popular Crescent Ballroom in downtown Seattle, on 6th Avenue between Pike and Pine, where it's dance time with **Lois Apple**, her piano and her men of music."

Dance remotes were staple radio fare in the 40's. Lois' announcer was husband Bill Apple. Her theme: "Apple Blossom Time," of course.

The good-natured Colonel used to joke about billing his big-city colleagues for running their training program.

The University of Washington, which *should* have been training up new blood for the industry, was still years away from an effective program. The "U" had fiddled some with radio back in the early twenties, running experimental station 7XZ for a couple of years, but apparently lost interest. Tom Herbert, barely out of school himself, was assigned to teach a class in radio acting beginning in 1936; but the only facility the "U" could give him was a makeshift studio in back of the men's room in the Meany Hall basement. It was surrounded by the cacophony of the School of Music's practice rooms.

Herbert, who at one time was Seattle's highest paid script writer, quit in ill-concealed disgust after about a

Nobody but "Colonel" **Leo Beckley** thought small-town radio was possible when he put **KBRC**, Mount Vernon, on the air in 1946 with just five employes. The Skagit Valley town was considered too small to support a radio station. But KBRC is still going strong, and here's Leo (on the left) getting a 25-year award from Seattle Bureau Chief **Marty Heerwald** of United Press-International.

Below: Announcer **Fred Grant** reads the morning news to listeners of **KBRC** back in 1949.

year. Ted Bell replaced him, just as the University decided to refit a dusty old experimental theater called the "Crow's Nest" into a radio studio. It was a primitive affair high up under the cupolas of Denny Hall. Ted taught the course there for the Drama Department until the later forties.

Ted also taught a class in writing radio plays, the English Department offered something called "Radio Speech," and you could take a course in radio news over at the Journalism building.

Eventually a red-headed English professor named Ed Adams was appointed to pull everything together in a single Radio Education Department. Studios and offices were built into a kind of glorified shack on the edge of the campus and pronounced "Radio Hall." Bruce Calhoun, by then one of the most experienced broadcasters in the area, was hired to run the operation and accent the professional as opposed to the theoretical.

Radio Hall produced a dozen or so educational programs on discs which were aired over cooperating stations around the state. Adams' own "Reading for Fun," a book review show, was a typical offering.

Then there was a children's theater program, produced and directed by a pretty young teacher named Ruth Prins—the future Wunda Wunda.

Seattle's Mayor **Gordon Clinton** did so many radio and TV broadcasts to the community he offered to join AFTRA, the broadcasters' union. AFTRA's officers made him an honorary member instead. In this ceremony (around 1960) AFTRA secretary **George Peckham** (left), broadcast veteran **Tom Herbert**, and local union President **Bill Schonely** (white jacket) present Clinton with his membership certificate as **Bruce Calhoun**, a charter member of AFTRA, looks on.

144

The University of Washington's Radio Hall crew, about 1949. From left: **Bruce Calhoun**, **Ed Adams**, **Ken Kager**, and **Al Roberts**.

Ed Adams (left) prepares to interview author **Betty McDonald** (right) on his "Reading for Fun" radio show out of Radio Hall on the University of Washington campus. Also present are **Bruce Calhoun** and **Mrs. Adams**.

(University of Washington)

KUOW's FM antenna going up on top of Johnson Hall near Radio Hall on the University of Washington campus, towards the end of 1951.

Ken Kager of **KUOW** instructing University of Washington student **Dick Priest** at the FM station's operating console.

Early in 1950 another FM station came on the air in Seattle. Ellwood Lippincott's KISW was, in its first years, a super-low budget operation. The station was located in a small concrete building at 9201 Roosevelt Way, the antenna bolted to a wooden pole in the front yard. As one means of filling air time at no cost, Manager Jack Hemingway made a deal to carry several hours of programming direct from Radio Hall each week.

Two years later KUOW was born, as Radio Hall came on the air—but just barely. The 1,000-watt transmitter (not much power on FM) and an antenna that never would load up properly were installed at nearby Johnson Hall. Few could hear the station except right in Seattle's north end.

Then KING's Mrs. Bullitt came to the rescue, donating a 10-kW transmitter and antenna. This equipment (actually the gift was to the Seattle Public Schools) was removed from its Smith Tower location, lowered some 21 floors to the street and reassembled at the Edison Technical School. Edison's Nick Foster and his students operated the transmitter from that time, with programming still provided by the University. Now, KUOW's coverage area included all of Western Washington and then some. For a time it was the most powerful non-commercial FM station in the country.

Meanwhile the FCC's freeze on TV station construction had ended, with new rules setting aside channels for educational television. In due course the state legislature scheduled a hearing on the feasibility of funding such an outlet in the Puget Sound area. That's just what Bruce Calhoun, along with assistants Ken Kager and Al Roberts, had been advocating for years. But their superiors at the "U" weren't interested. Calhoun discovered they weren't even planning to send a spokesman!

When Bruce stopped ricocheting off the plywood walls of Radio Hall he went right to the top, gaining authorization from President Raymond Allen himself to testify in Olympia.

There were other speakers there, from some of the commercial stations, and they were mostly opposed. They didn't fancy the competition. But Calhoun spoke eloquently in favor of public TV, and at length the legislature made the appropriation.

So, almost grudgingly, the "U" finally joined with other colleges, public schools and libraries to establish KCTS (**K**ing **C**ounty **T**elevision **S**ervice) on Channel 9. The studio was housed, at first, in another ancient portable next to Radio Hall. Mrs. Bullitt donated the transmitter—it was Channel 5's original—and students at Edison Technical School, where it was to be housed and operated, converted it to the higher frequency.

"¿Qué es eso?" Here "Doña Mercedes" (**Olga Mercedes Ramona Rojas Castañeda de Edgerton**) uses a doll house and furniture to teach a Spanish lesson. Note mirror which, with another mirror out of the picture at the top, provides cameras with a down-view of the house.

Channel 9 studio in the early 60's. Here Professor **Milo Ryan** (center, with glasses) and students in his television production class confer prior to taping a project. Students (from left) are **Gordon Thorne**, **Gary Tubesing** and **Ella Henrickson**.

Ryan was founder of the University's unique Phonoarchive of vintage radio recordings. (See Appendix.)

With Channel 9 on the air at last, there was just one more VHF slot still unoccupied in Seattle: the much contested channel 7. For years that spot on everyone's dial had been and would remain dark, while KVI, KXA and KIRO kept up their tenacious battle of legal briefs, hearings, challenges and replies, each hoping ultimately to get the FCC's official nod.

True, Saul Haas' political clout had diminished considerably since the old days. But the smart money was betting on Saul all the same, and the smart money was right. In 1957 the Commission awarded the precious license to KIRO, which announced it would begin telecasting the following February 8.

Suddenly CBS announced, notwithstanding its contract with Channel 11, it would switch to KIRO-TV the same day.

KTNT-TV screamed "foul," went to court and demanded 15 million dollars' treble-damages under the anti-trust laws.

It didn't collect. But neither did the Tacoma station go broke. Building its schedule around movies, sports and "syndications," KTNT-TV survived. Since then the call letters have been changed (to KSTW, for Seattle-Tacoma, Washington), there is a new owner, and the station has moved into big, flashy new quarters brimming with futuristic equipment; but that same magic formula continues to keep the accountants grinning. In fact, KSTW has become one of the top money-makers in the Puget Sound market.

Amazing, what you can do with reruns.

KIRO, Inc. President and General Manager **Lloyd Cooney**, well known in the Puget Sound country as the opinionated promulgator of forthright—and usually controversial—broadcast editorials. Cooney left the station in 1980 to enter politics.

One of **KIRO-TV**'s early shows was "Andy and Sport," a live comedy starring **Craig Shreeve** (left) as the restaurant owner and **Chris Wedes** (better known for his role as "J. P. Patches") as the bumbling Greek-accented chef.

Guest **Lola Hallowell** breaks up as J. P. Patches interviews her in honor of National Secretary Week. Lola was a **KIRO-TV** secretary when the station went on the air in 1958.

1973 celebration for **KIRO-TV**'s J. P. Patches. Here **Chris Wedes**, who plays the durable clown, is honored by old friends: (from left) **Bill Mudge**, **Bill Gerald**, **Stan Boreson**, and **Don McCune**. Mudge and Gerald used to work on the show. Boreson and McCune formerly had competing programs on Channels 5 and 4, respectively.

CHAPTER TEN

Mr. Baseball

Back in the summer of 1921 young Carl Haymond, the ex-World War sailor and radioman, was still pounding Seattle's hilly streets in search of decent work. He was married now, and trying to remember how it was to afford proper food three times a day.

Then he saw the ad.

The Post-Intelligencer wanted somebody to run their new radio station. Applicants needed a pleasant voice, a college degree, and a valid license. Haymond qualified all three ways and was soon reporting for duty at the P-I.

His first announcing assignment was that famous Dempsey-Carpentier fight re-creation which, as we have seen, opened the radio age along Puget Sound. The broadcast also established Carl Haymond as the area's trailblazing sportscaster.

In October, Haymond broadcast the World Series games, again relying on bulletins of the International News Service ticker. Somehow the arrangements didn't get made in time for the opening contest, but Haymond was at his microphone for the rest of the games. (It was an exciting Series. The New York Giants creamed the Yankees, for once, five games to three.)

The World Series broadcasts were repeated yearly on the station. By 1924, though, the telegraphers had their act together and were sending the action play-by-play, with Haymond's word pictures hitting the air seconds behind the actual game. His descriptions were so graphic, listeners-in almost felt they were sitting right in the stands.

That was the year the P-I station went permanently silent and Carl Haymond moved over to the Rhodes store as manager of KFOA. He had barely settled into the job when he learned 2,000 fez-topped Masons of the Northwest Grotto Association were meeting in Seattle and planning a colorful procession down Second Avenue, right past the store.

The parade was to be led by a celebrated group of aviators and their flying machines.

Haymond figured he just had to get that on the air, but how? Finally he gathered up all the spare wire he could find, pieced it together into one long extension cord, and climbed out onto the arcade roof with his microphone.

The broadcast went so well, Haymond was seized by an audacious thought. Football season had arrived, and the University of Washington was about to play host to the Montana Grizzlies. Why not rent a telephone company line all the way out to Husky Stadium and broadcast that game right from the field?

And that's just what he did. Sitting all alone in the stands before his primitive carbon mike, and with the cheers of the fans adding to the drama of that historic broadcast, he described all the abundant action as Washington trounced Montana 52 to 7.

It was an exhausting feat. Later, sportscasters would be flanked by spotters, engineers, and sidekick announcers to handle the commercials and color. But Carl Haymond did all of that himself, that Saturday in 1924 when live sportscasting was born on the shores of Lake Washington.

But Haymond was busying himself with the business end of radio, and soon other voices were becoming familiar to sports fans of the later twenties. Art Chamberlin. Bob Nichols. Al Schuss. Ken Fisher remembers when he, Nichols and Harold "Tubby" Quilliam (later manager of KIRO) broadcast Husky crew races for the first time in the spring of 1927.

Schuss was still at the height of his own career as an all-Coast college basketball star, under the legendary "Hec" Edmundson, when he began broadcasting for KJR in 1928. He later became sports director for the station. Then he went back East, changed his name to Alan Hale and broadcast Brooklyn Dodgers' games as "Red" Barber's sidekick.

Another enormously popular announcer around 1930 was handsome, moon-faced Ken Stuart, whose smooth tenor voice was one of the busiest in Seattle. Stuart parted his dark hair almost exactly in the middle, and sported a bright red necktie as his personal trademark. On a nightly program called "Sunshine" he sang sentimental and inspirational warbles, read poetry of the Edgar Guest variety, and chatted intimately with an audience that ran largely to middle-aged females.

His theme song was that old workhorse of all Irish tenors, "When You're Smiling."

Stuart was one of those who stayed on KJR, following that station's first bankruptcy in 1929. In the lean times that followed he would find ways to plead his poverty over the air, and listeners would send him gifts of food and other needed items. When his wife Dotty became pregnant, he mentioned that fact and was showered with baby things.

One of Stuart's sons has since traced his dad's footsteps, by the way. Ken Stuart Jr. became a prominent announcer on Seattle stations during the fifties and sixties. He tired of the grind, though, and currently runs a small country store in the Eastern Washington town of Conconully.

Seattle's **Al Schuss** interviews heavyweight boxing champ **Joe Lewis**. Schuss, a one-time basketball star under "Hec" Edmundson at the University of Washington, was an early sports announcer for **KJR**. He then went back east and, as "Alan Hale," broadcast baseball games with the likes of Walter Lanier "Red" Barber. Later, Schuss returned to the coast and became the radio voice of the San Diego Padres.

Bob Nichols, who started in broadcasting as a singer over the Seattle P-I's pioneer radio station in 1921, became a well-known sportscaster in the later 20's. He is shown here in a publicity pose for **KJR**, where he was sports director.

The senior Stuart was also chief sports announcer at KJR and covered a busy schedule of live football, crew, hockey, dog races, boxing and wrestling events. He was at his best describing wrestling, but sometimes got carried away. Once, when a pair of grunt-and-groaners were mixing it up pretty good, he screamed into his mike: "He's killing him! Call an ambulance!" And listeners took him seriously. In moments, seven ambulances converged on the arena.

Stuart broadcast an occasional baseball game on KJR but it was 1931 before a local station was prevailed on to carry a full schedule of Seattle Indians ball games. Attendance was off at Dugdale Park, and "Bald Bill" Klepper, who owned the team, was trying to whip up more interest. He even hired a press

Robert Bruce Hesketh, all-around star athlete and a glamor figure in the Pacific Northwest in the 1920s. Hesketh was picked to broadcast Seattle baseball games beginning in 1931. When he didn't make the grade, a young sports writer named Leo Lassen took over and was launched on a legendary career. (Oddly enough, the two men were neighbors in Seattle's north end.)

agent—a certain unemployed newspaperman with a predilection for derby hats and a voice like a faulty chain saw.

KXA carried the games and the announcer was to be Bob Hesketh, one of the Northwest's most glamorous athletes of all time. Hesketh had so many sports letters from Lincoln High School days he'd been written up in Ripley's "Believe It Or Not." His clear, resonant voice was perfect for radio, too. He knew baseball, he was enthusiastic, and he was good.

There was just one problem.

Hesketh was a product of the Lost Generation, one of the twenties' "flaming youth" whose idea of a good time was to hit every speakeasy in town as often as possible. By 1931, tragically, he was an alcoholic. A month into the season, he'd already missed several broadcasts. He was canned, and went back to his old job—selling cars for a living.

Then one or two other announcers were given a try. They had great voices, too. But they just couldn't make the games come alive. Klepper would patrol the back of the park's rickety press box, listening to the cutesie drivel pouring from the radio side of the enclosure, and shake his head.

"Strikey oney," said a hopeful at one point, and it was the last straw. In desperation Klepper turned to his press agent and asked if he wouldn't please take a crack at it.

He did, and a legend was born.

Some three decades and 70-odd million words later, Leo Harvey Lassen's name and his shrill, rapid-fire delivery would be familiar in virtually every household on Puget Sound. He was to become the best-known and most respected sports announcer on the West Coast, and just possibly the Pacific Northwest's most outstanding radio personality of all time.

Leo spent virtually his whole life in Seattle. He was born just before the century's turn to Peter A. and Minnie Lassen, who came West to Everett in 1901 and moved to Seattle soon afterward. They lived at 812 Motor Place, a few steps from Aurora Avenue. Leo attended B. F. Day grade school and graduated from Lincoln High in 1917. He was an only child.

Leo couldn't play baseball himself. His left arm, broken in a youthful roller skating accident, was slightly crippled. (He used to claim the doctor was drunk when he set it.) All his life Leo carried that arm tucked in closely to his side, and he was forever dropping things, even packs of cigarettes, out of his left hand.

The handicap kept him from playing baseball, but—curiously—not his other passion, which was the piano. He loved music and would play classics by the hour, from memory—what Fuzzy Hufft, a Seattle outfielder, once called "them society marches."

Leo's was a complex personality. He certainly didn't suffer much from diffidence. His nickname was "Pest" at Lincoln, where, his senior annual discloses, he "rather hesitatingly" ranked himself "a little below Paderewski" as a piano player.

154

Alex Shults, the sports writer, used to call him "the Great Gabbo."

Yet Leo was an intensely private person. He had just a few close friends. He never married. He was engaged once, but that was back at the start of the Depression and Leo couldn't afford a wife. By the time he could, his one-and-only had married somebody else. So Leo lived with his mother, as long as she lived, and she lived to be 98.

Oddly enough Minnie Lassen's voice was a carbon copy of her famous son's. It was pitched a bit higher, but there was no mistaking that metallic timbre, like unoiled gears, and the relentless machine-gun delivery. In conversation their combined—and generally simultaneous—decibels shook the very walls and quickly reduced any third parties present to an awed silence.

For hobbies, Leo grew roses and wrote poems. They were pretty good poems, too. Here's one he penned while in a wistful mood one Christmas season:

THE SACRED HOUR

They said he never knew the joys
Of little children, trees and toys
On Christmas day;
And that he always was alone—
He had no kinsfolk of his own
To join in play.
But when the cloak of evening falls
And fire lights the shadowed walls
With amber gleam,
He lives a sacred hour of mirth,
A child again before the hearth—
A treasured dream.
And there he builds his Christmas tree
In all its tinseled mystery.

Alone. But they will never know
The tryst with dreams of yesterday
He keeps within the embers' glow
Where flame and shadow dance and play.*

Leo had wanted to go to college, but his father, a Fremont destrict shingle mill foreman, died while he was at Lincoln. So he went to work after graduation, as an office boy at the Post-Intelligencer. He landed a job the following year as a reporter for the old Seattle Star.

A few months more and Leo, just twenty, was promoted to sports editor.

He wrote in an aggressive, flamboyant manner, garnishing his columns with stunning circumlocution. Base hits were base "knocks," outfielders were "orchard men," the ball was a "pill" or "agate." Batters were "swatsmiths" or "stickers." First base was the "initial pillow."

* More poetry by Leo Lassen will be found in the Appendix.

A rare photo of **Leo Lassen** as a schoolboy, still in short pants. He poses here with his mother, **Minnie Lassen**, with whom Leo continued to live until her death at 98 years of age.

Describing a Salt Lake City ballpark, he once wrote that "the Mormon town's left field fence" was "shorter than a winter day in the arctic zone."

He could be pretty caustic in those salad days. After one week of unspectacular ball-playing he observed that "Seattle hasn't lost so many games in Los Angeles—only seven. It could have lost more, perhaps, but that is all the games the schedule called for at the Angel hangout."

Leo mellowed a good deal through the twenties. Just before the Depression hit he was promoted to managing editor of the Star.

Just *after* the Depression hit he was fired, along with almost everybody else on the paper.

For a year or two he was just a journalist. (Which, his friend Alex Shults observed, really means "newspaperman out of work.") That's when Leo signed up to do public relations work for the Seattle team, which led subsequently to Bill Klepper's invitation to take over the baseball microphone.

Tigers Step Into First Place; Other Gossip of Baseball Here and There

George Kelly and Leo Strait Star in the International League; Will Tigers Hold Lead on Road? Seattle Squad Invades Salt Lake Next Week; Club Home for Month Stay in August.

BY LEO H. LASSEN

Shades of Nero! Cans't believe what thou lampest! Just take another glimpse at that standing of the Coast league clubs today and wonder why the exclamation. Y'see the Vernon Tigers are leading the Coast league procession for the first time this season and the Los Angeles tribe is looking up at another club for the initial performance since the race got under way.

Who would have ever dreamed that the Angels' magnificent lead would dwindle to nothingness within the course of a couple of weeks? In fact, one terrible week with Vernon in Los Angeles and the first four days of the Sacramento series spelt second money for the Angels.

The road wrecked the Angels and in spite of all the help the Seraphs were handed by the schedule makers, who allowed the Angels to play 10 out of the first 11 weeks at home, the Angels are in second place today. This is not predicting that Vernon will win the pennant, because that Los Angeles crew has its heart set on bringing home the rag and they have one powerful ball crew.

The next four weeks will decide the Coast race beyond a doubt. Vernon goes on the road for a month's jaunt next week. Will the Tigers be able to hold up? If the jungle tribe can take the trip around the Northern end of the circuit and survive they should romp home. The schedule, however, again favors the Angels to regain their lead as they are on their home lot for a month's stay while the Tigers are roaming about.

Tigers Here Soon

The Tigers will be in Seattle in three weeks. Whether or not "Fatty" Arbuckle, the movie comedian, who pilots the Tigers, will head his tribe here is uncertain now, but one thing is sure, and that is if he does come the park won't be able to hold the fans.

Before coming to Seattle the Tigers open in Oakland and then jump to

Old Hans Wagner Was Some Player, Yodels Muggsy

"I consider Hans Wagner the most valuable all around player who ever wore a spiked shoe."

High School Mentor Returns to Lincoln

Ernie Wells

This is Ernie Wells, local high school athletic coach, who will return to his old post at Lincoln high school next fall, after an absence of two years, part of which time was spent in the training camp at the Presidio, and part as a war worker in France. He coached at Queen Anne during the past spring.

Wells is one of the most popular athletic mentors who ever held down such a job in local high school circles. He made his reputation as a football coach and turned out many winners at the North End institution. He has his men playing the game all of the time, and is loved by his men for playing the game, and playing it clean.

Thru the Ropes

Frankie Murphy, Coast flyweight king, leaves for Los Angeles the first of the month. Frankie will make his home in the South. He has notified the San Francisco promoters that he is coming, and expects to land a couple of scraps at the Golden Gate where he plans to

Home Runs Sixth Wall Seattle Cr

Borton and Fisher H Out Circuit Clouts in Frame; Murphy Sta

How Coast Clubs Sta

	Won.	Lo
Vernon	61	4
Los Angeles	62	44
San Francisco	57	4
Salt Lake City	55	4
Sacramento	47	55
Oakland	48	55
Portland	44	56
Seattle	37	61

LOS ANGELES, July 26 same old comedy was enacte yesterday, when the Vernon Tigers, 4 t before the best game of the week's se

Two home runs, planted two doubles wrecked the Seatt for the fourth straight time, all happened in the sixth when Borton and Fisher ham out home run wallops after and High had doubled.

Seattle squeezed over a run eighth frame, but the North were never dangerous. M playing shortstop for the vi clicked out three hits for th and led the hitters.

Brenton pitched a good game the exception of the sixth i when things happened so q that the war was over befor Seattle crew realized it. D held the visitors to three bing

Seatle—	AB.	R.	H.	PO.
Schaller, rf	4	0	0	2
Cunningham, cf	4	0	0	
Walsh, 1b	4	0	0	16
Compton, lf	3	0	0	2
Perring, 3b	4	0	0	0
Lapan, c	4	0	0	
Hosp, 2b	3	0	0	0
Murphy, ss	3	1	3	1
Brenton, p	3	0	1	1
Totals	32	1	4	24
Vernon—	AB.	R.	H.	PO.
Mitchell, ss	4	0	0	1
Chadbourne, cf	4	1	1	3
Meusel, 3b	4	1	1	0
Borton, 1b	3	1	2	14

A 1919 column by Seattle Star sports reporter **Leo Lassen**. The future broadcaster was barely 20 years old. "Lamp" that flamboyant writing style!

His first broadcast was an out-of-town contest, a re-creation. A skilled young Morse operator named "Hap" Garthright set up his apparatus in KXA's transmitter room. Announcer Earl Thoms sat Leo at a wicker table in the small, ornately carpeted studio adjoining, and after signing the broadcast on the air, kept busy hustling little five-by-seven-inch slips of pink paper to him from the telegrapher.

Play-by-play reporting of distant ball games came under Paragraph One of Western Union's Commercial News Department. Only the essential information was transmitted, in a kind of shorthand: S1C for "Strike one called," B1 HI for "Ball one high," and so on. It was left to the announcer's imagination, intuition and general knowledge of baseball to supply all the rest:

the color, the repartee between players and umpires, all that essential trivia about batters tugging at their caps and pitchers glancing at first base before the windup.

(Either you were good at this sort of thing or you weren't. Back in Des Moines, there was a slender chap named "Dutch" Reagan who used to re-create ball games that way. He did so well he went from radio to the movies and then to politics. His first name, by the way, is Ronald.)

Leo was mighty good at it, right from that first day. Because he didn't have to invent much. He *knew* what was going on at the distant diamond, because he knew the players so well. He knew their mannerisms, their weak and strong points, each pitcher's favorite strategy.

Convicted bootlegger Roy Olmstead's radio station was purchased by Vincent Kraft in 1926. After several call letter changes it became **KXA**, with this studio in the Bigelow Building, Fourth and Pike Street, Seattle. Leo Lassen's first baseball broadcast originated here, at the wicker table, in 1931.

Leo Lassen, one-time Seattle Star sports writer and newsman. Leo is shown here around the time of his debut, in 1931, as a baseball broadcaster.

And he had phenomenal concentration: when he described a long fly, Earl Thoms recalls, Leo's eyes would rise in the small, airless studio as though they were following a real ball in an actual park.

He wasn't even nervous. But he did keep his hat on all the time, and he played with the brim a lot. (The hat became his talisman. Leo would never broadcast without one—though in later years he switched from the derby to a light-weight straw or Panama.)

Baseball broadcasts were a shaky proposition at first. There wasn't much money in it. Sponsors, when you could find them, took an inning or two apiece and paid off in merchandise. The games kept changing from station to station.

There were times when Leo dipped into his own pocket to pay Western Union tolls, just to keep baseball on the air.

Once he and Hap arrived to do a game over KVL, a small record station on top of the Benjamin Franklin Hotel, and found the door locked. Nobody answered their knocking, so Hap climbed out on a ledge and entered the station through an outside window. Then he let Leo in the door, hooked up his key and clicker and started "taking" the game.

About then an operator emerged from the control room and said the broadcast was cancelled. He wasn't supposed to let Leo in, that's why the door was locked, and he had better leave. Leo refused. Hap kept copying the ball game.

First half of the third inning of a ball game between the Seattle Indians and Oakland Acorns, at Oakland, June 10, 1936. This is how the telegraphic report would look to announcer Leo Lassen. From this sparse information Leo would recreate a masterpiece of color and excitement, filling in details partly from his imagination but mostly from his vast knowledge of the game and its players.

```
THIRD SEATTLE:

MULLER UP-   S1F.  B1 HI.  OUT.   MULLER FLIED TO GLYNN IN RIGHT CENTER.

SMITH UP-   S1C.  S2F.  B1 LO OS.   S3F.  OUT.  SMITH FANNED.

GREGORY UP-   B1 HI.  B2 HI OS.  B3 HIGH.  S1C.  S2C.  B4 HI INSIDE.
GREGORY WALKED.

DONOVAN UP-   B1 LO OS.  PTF.  B2 LO.  PTF.  S1F.  B3 HI OS.  PTF.  B4 LO.
DONOVAN WALKED..  GREGORY ON SECOND.

BONETTI UP- S1F.  S2F.  B1 LO OS.  S3C.  OUT.  BONETTI OUT ON A CALLED
THIRD STRIKE.

          NO RUNS   NO HITS   NO ERRORS   TWO LEFT..
```

Then station manager Art Dailey showed up, mad as hell, saying his bill for air time hadn't been paid. Leo said it had. Hap kept on copying.

There was a terrible row, but Leo held his ground, and at length the game went on the air. Next day, though, there was a scramble to find another radio station by air time. And so it went in the thirties.

Some stations delayed out-of-town game re-creations by a few hours, due to conflicts with sponsored programs. This led to other kinds of conflicts. Leo might just be getting underway with some thrilling first inning action when an overzealous announcer would interrupt excitedly:

"A late bulletin from Sacramento, sports fans! The Indians have just lost to the Solons, sixteen to two!"

On smaller stations there were frequent delays to fix dilapidated equipment that kept breaking down. And one station broke into the game regularly each day to plug a headache remedy for fifteen minutes.

(Seattle Times)

Leo Lassen about 1940, near the height of his career. Times sports writer Alex Shults figured "Gabbo" had broadcast 24 million high-pitched words to date.

Arthur C. Dailey was owner, manager, and chief engineer of **KVL**, Seattle. An avid experimenter, he used to retune his broadcast transmitter to amateur radio frequencies after sign-off and use it as a "ham" station. Here he tries out a two-way short wave set built into the back of his 1938 Terraplane.

Dailey was a pleasant, easy-going employer. When the station was on top of the Spring Apartment Hotel, operators would even ask to work there for nothing. Perhaps the fact that the control room window overlooked the YWCA shower room had something to do with that.

(Seattle Historical Society)

H. C. "Hap" Garthright was Leo Lassen's telegrapher during much of the great sportscaster's broadcasting career. Hap is shown here with his wife **Marie**. She too was a Western Union operator in those days.

For many years, besides broadcasting games, Leo wrote them up for the P-I. One Sunday afternoon there occurred a spectacular beef between "Dutch" Reuther —a Seattle pitcher—and an umpire. Reuther lost his cool, stomped with his spikes on the umpire's foot, and got thrown out of the game. A little later he showed up in front of the radio box and during a break in the broadcast asked Leo to keep the incident out of the paper.

"Can't do it, Dutch," Leo told him deadpan. "It's news, you know."

Reuther kept insisting. And getting madder and madder. Finally he was clawing at the wire screen that separated them, threatening to tear Leo apart.

But there really wasn't anything Leo could do by then—because he'd already phoned in the story! Moments later, newsboys came clambering down the stands hawking garish extras with screaming headlines: REUTHER ATTACKS UMPIRE!

It was quite another matter, though, when Leo's own cherished privacy was intruded on. Once while re-creating a game at KRSC, he became aware of several young lady visitors to the station who were watching him through the control room window. Distracted, he failed to see one of the telegrapher's slips fall to the floor and he omitted an entire inning from the broadcast.

Naturally there was consternation among Leo's audience, but nothing like the consternation at the station where it was learned Alex Shults wanted to write up "Leo's missing inning" for the Times. Hap Garthright finally talked Alex out of it, and Leo got the station owner to install curtains on his window.

There was panic at KJR, too, the day Garthright showed up to take a Sunday double-header and found the staff standing around the hallway wringing their hands. Because, they said, "Leo refuses to go on." It turned out Alex Shults had put a feature article and picture of Leo's mother in the paper, and Leo was furious.

"That's our private life, dammit, Hap," he growled. It took a while, but Garthright finally convinced him the article was really a compliment (which it was) and Leo calmed down and did the broadcast.

Because of such incidents, he was often considered a kind of prima donna. Actually, Leo was a sensitive artist who took his job seriously. Yet something there was that invited persecution. One Fourth of July at Civic Field, reporters tossed a firecracker under his chair. The blast wrecked the microphone, all but shell-shocked Leo, and made a shambles of the broadcast.

It was several days before he regained his composure, and there were rumors Leo was acting strangely and might have to be "put away."*

By the late nineteen-thirties, baseball had become extremely popular the length of Puget Sound. Sure, Emil Sick bought the Indians and made them the Rainiers, and built a fine stadium out in the valley. But it was largely Leo's doing, too. He had so many fans, you could walk down some streets of a warm summer evening and not miss a play: the familiar rasp of his voice reached you through doorway after doorway.

Even a lackluster contest contained elements of drama to keep his listeners spellbound. "The game is never over till the last man is out," Leo would intone

---

* Not that Leo was the only sportscaster to get picked on. Ted Husing and Bill Stern, announcing for rival networks, used to arrive for broadcasts and find their mike cables cut, press box doors nailed shut, and so on.

gravely, and you sensed the hope—though Seattle trailed by six runs at the last of the ninth. With a closer finish (two men on base, say, with two away and the three-two pitch coming up) his voice would rise whole octaves with excitement. "Hang onto those rocking chairs!" he demanded then—as though our knuckles weren't already white with holding on.

He was a past master at timing and suspense. The rhythm of his delivery, the length of a pause, the underplayed touch of surprise or irony in his voice were all part of the skillful orchestration: Leo the musician at work. When he told you Mount Rainier was a big ice cream cone looking down on Sick's Stadium, or the rising moon was "peeking over the right field fence like a big ball of fire," that was Leo the poet talking.

He didn't just put you in the stands with his description; he put you right in the game. "If you've never been hit by a foul tip you don't know what you've missed," he liked to remind us when the catcher grappled with a sizzler, and our own fingertips were sure to smart a little.

(Broadcast Pioneers Library)

Ted Husing was just a so-so staff announcer on CBS when Bill Paley took over the struggling network in 1927. Then Paley sent him to substitute for ailing sportscaster J. Andrew White one day, and a star, as they say, was born. Here the great Husing broadcasts from Yankee Stadium in New York during radio's heyday.

But that was frosting. The cake was Leo's flawless knowledge of baseball. He drilled us in the strategies of the game. He explained the infield fly rule so even grandmothers and maiden aunts could understand. (He was also the Seattle team's unofficial "manager." After a game he would come down to the locker room and post-mortem: How come you did this? Why didn't you do that? And of course, he was usually right.)

And Leo was accurate. If he reported that Mike Hunt had switched his chaw of cut plug from his right cheek to his left ("We bring you *all* the news!") or the umpire was making three passes over the plate with his little broom ("Swish, swish, swish") you knew that's precisely what happened.

(It wasn't always that way with sportscasters. NBC's Bill Stern came to Seattle once for a Big Ten football game. Gazing out from Husky Stadium past the sanitary landfill to reedy Union Bay, he waxed positively rhapsodic for his nationwide audience over the grandeurs of the "blue Pacific." And Stern couldn't always remember the players' numbers. If he made a mistake identifying the ball carrier, somebody would nudge him, and he'd invent a "lateral pass" to get the ball back in the right hands.)*

Even when re-creating games by wire, Leo was always nagging his telegraphers for "more color." One day one of them regaled him with a sarcastic and long-winded description of a knot-hole in the left field fence when a home run ball passed over it.

Hap Garthright, on the receiving end of the wire through much of Leo's career, would sometimes sweeten otherwise sparse accounts with a few details of his own invention. But Leo wasn't fooled. "You know, Hap," he said one time, "it looks like there are three different games going on here. The one down in California, the one you're giving me, and the one I'm putting on the air!"

On occasion the operator down south would finish a game, get in his car and listen to Leo's version of the last inning as he drove home. It was a weird, *déjà vu* experience, what with the signal filtered and other-worldly over the skywave reception, and Leo coming across so believably with details that the telegrapher had never sent him.

* Stern began his career as an usher, and later stage manager, at "Roxy" Rothafel's New York theater. He always considered himself a showman rather than a reporter. Dramatic sports stories he told on the top-rated "Cavalcade of Sports" radio show were scandalously embellished with fictional details of his own invention. Yet, he was for years America's top sportscaster—in every sport but horse racing. And Clem McCarthy once quipped *that* was only because "You can't lateral a horse."

(University of Washington)

Seattle announcer **Ted Bell** broadcast Husky football games for many years. Six-feet-four, and weighing in the two hundreds, Bell had played the game himself in high school and college days. He was an excellent announcer, but did tend to make unfortunate ad-libs: "He caught that pass rather high—about where he'd wear a necklace!" Only in those days men didn't wear necklaces. And certainly not football players.

A youthful **Tom Bean** got into radio right out of high school during the war. Bean worked at KRKO, Everett, then moved to KRSC in Seattle where he became Leo Lassen's announcer.

162

Leo Lassen broadcasting from the radio booth of Sick's Stadium in 1951. (Seattle Times photo by Don Duncan.)

KRSC carried the games through much of the forties, with alternate sponsorship by Wheaties ("The Breakfast of Champions!") and Goodrich tires. Ted Bell was Leo's sidekick. One day a left-hander named Lou Tost was pitching, and "Coffee Joe" Coscarart was at third base. During a pause in the action, Ted ad-libbed that with Coffee and Tost in the lineup, "All we need now is some ham and eggs and we'll have the perfect breakfast."

There was a stunning four-beat silence. Nobody needed television to visualize the two announcers staring at one another in dismay. Finally came Leo's voice, underplaying, almost casual. "Of course," he observed, "this is Goodrich's day. So we're not *supposed* to mention Wheaties."

Not too long after that, Leo had a new sidekick. But maybe that was coincidence. Television was coming in. Ted moved over to the new medium, and became the Northwest's pioneer video sports personality.

There was a question, when that big red eye blinked on at last, whether Leo or the camera could transmit the more vivid picture of a ball game. Apparently nobody at Channel 5 thought seriously of hiring Leo away from radio. And the result was wholly predictable. Thousands watched on the tube, but instead of listening to KING's Bill O'Mara, they turned down the TV sound and tuned in Leo on the radio, just like before.

KRSC-TV cameramen in action at Sick's Stadium in Seattle, 1949.

KING-TV sportscaster **Bill O'Mara** called many a hydroplane race in TV's early years, along with other sports events. It was O'Mara (whose real name is **Bill Rhodes**) who led his audience in the Lord's Prayer following the death of two hydro drivers during a 1951 race.

Only it wasn't like before, not really. And it never would be again. Little by little, TV was surely taking over. Old movies and new excitements were luring even Leo's fans away to the Big Eye. Like the Gold Cup hydroplane races that began in 1951. (That was the year "Quicksilver" flipped over in the third heat, breaking apart on thousands of little screens as televiewers watched in horror. Bill O'Mara, learning that two drivers were dead, knelt down on-camera and led his audience in prayer.)

By 1957 the end was in sight. Leo's contract expired and could not be renewed to his liking. For two years he stayed around his Latona Avenue home, caring for Minnie and his roses, while a young Montanan named Rod Belcher took over the radio mike.* Leo returned

* Rod had been broadcaster for the San Francisco Forty-Niners, using the name Rod Hughes. His sponsor—a now defunct beer company—didn't think "Belcher" was appropriate for their product.

164

Rod Belcher (right) with **Lindsey Nelson** broadcasting the Rose Bowl game in Pasadena, California, 1964. Belcher entered radio in Montana in 1942, came to the Northwest and was one of the University of Washington's football and basketball sportscasters for Tidewater Associated Oil Company (remember "Let's get Associated!" and "Flying-A Gas"?) along with Ted Bell, Pat Hayes and John Jarstad.

Belcher succeeded the legendary Leo Lassen as Seattle Rainiers baseball announcer in 1957, later became sports director for KING radio and TV in the 60's.

Al Smith (left) and **Earl Thoms** demonstrate the 40-inch telescopic lens they invented for **KING-TV**'s early Gold Cup race coverage. The side-mounted lens is actually an astronomical telescope using a home-ground 6-inch mirror, with smaller mirrors for coupling the image into the camera's pickup tube. Until telescopic Zoomar lenses came along, two different networks used this patented system, which grew out of Earl Thoms' longtime hobbies of lens-grinding and star-gazing.

Up, up, and over! When **Slo-Mo-Shun V** performed its unscheduled aerial loop far out on the back stretch of Lake Washington's Gold Cup course in 1955, cameraman Al Smith caught the surprise maneuver with **KING-TV**'s new telescope camera. The dramatic pictures, unprecedented in that era, were widely reprinted in newspapers and on national TV. Miraculously, driver Lou Fageol escaped serious injury.

to the air for two more seasons, over KOMO, and retired from broadcasting in 1960.

He never went back to the ballpark, never really watched or listened to another game. He declined interviews. The nearest he came to public appearances was a daily stroll to the corner grocery.

Leo died in December 1975, at Ballard Community Hospital, not a mile from his boyhood home. He had no known living relatives (Minnie died in 1968) and just a handful of friends.

Yet hundreds turned out in a cold rain for his funeral. A few were long-time acquaintances: neighbors, gray-haired newsmen, former ball players. But most were just fans—middle-aged to old, mostly—who didn't forget, though Leo hadn't faced a microphone in fifteen years.

And there was no stopping the tears when the organist played Leo's old theme song, "Take Me Out to the Ball Game." They'd heard it so many times before. But not as they heard it now: slowly, softly, poignantly. A farewell dirge for Leo Lassen, "Mr. Baseball," whose like we'll surely not know again.

(Seattle Times)

Leo Lassen, Seattle's baseball broadcaster-legend, tending roses in retirement. He lived here, on Latona Avenue in Seattle's Wallingford district, from 1929 until his death in 1975.

KIRO's heavyweight sportscaster **Wayne Cody**. A great Leo Lassen fan, Wayne has produced a fascinating record album of excerpts from Leo's baseball broadcasts. (See Appendix for information.)

CHAPTER ELEVEN

"The Voice of Seattle"

Early in 1926 Judge Jeremiah Neterer in Seattle sentenced Roy Olmstead, the rum-running "king," to four years in the McNeil Island penitentiary. Olmstead's conviction on liquor conspiracy charges had, however, been secured quite illegally. Unlawful wiretap evidence had been flagrantly used against him. Even the prosecutor was pretty sure the government's testimony was largely perjured.

The case was appealed all the way to the U.S. Supreme Court and Olmstead was so sure the Court would free him, he was already planning his re-entry into the broadcasting business. A young friend of his, Francis Brott, applied for a license and the call sign KXRO; and everyone understood the last two letters were really Roy's initials, and that the station would revert to him once the conviction was quashed.

In 1928, though, the Supreme Court split 5 to 4 against Olmstead, who went to prison until pardoned by President Roosevelt when Prohibition ended. (Olmstead became a convert to Christian Science while in prison, and devoted the rest of his life to serving the less fortunate.)

Francis Brott was a talented ham operator who augmented income from his regular job as a chauffeur by building high-quality receivers for local stations to use as monitors. About the time the license for KXRO came through, he dropped by the Fisher company's plant to see if the new KOMO, which they were then feverishly building, needed a monitor.

It turned out that what they really needed was another engineer.

Brott rolled up his sleeves then and there, gave up chauffeuring and became chief engineer of the big, new station. So what to do with KXRO? Brott simply handed it over to Olmstead's lieutenant, Al Hubbard.

Hubbard moved the station to Aberdeen, where—it was alleged in yet another liquor trial—he used it to signal booze boats off the Gray's Harbor bar.

KXRO's studio was on the top floor of Aberdeen's Finch Building, at South H and Heron Streets. The five-story structure was owned by the brothers Goodbar and Rogan Jones, whose insurance, real estate and loan company was on the ground floor. Government agents finally shut the station down, Hubbard went broke, and Jones & Jones—being the principal creditor—found they had a radio station on their hands.

Lafayette Rogan Jones, short, feisty, Tennessee-born, was going to write the whole thing off when a fellow named Harry Spence drove down from Tacoma to see him. Spence had been working for Carl Haymond and knew something about the business of broadcasting. If it was run right, he said, the station could make a pile of money.

That was Rogan's song. He told Spence to give it a try for ninety days, and if there was a profit, the two would become partners.

Three months later Rogan was an enthusiastic convert. He and Spence formed a company, not just to run KXRO but to look around for more stations they could pick up cheaply and turn into money machines. Traveling to Bellingham, they looked over KVOS, a little 100-watter that had gone broke, and made a deal with the bankruptcy court to take it over.

Then they bought a controlling interest in Moritz Thomsen's struggling KPCB, and picked up another all-but-defunct Seattle outlet, KPQ, to add to their string. KPCB stayed in Seattle. KPQ was moved to Wenatchee. The date was July 27, 1929.

In a few months the national economy was in disarray, most of their advertisers were broke, and the young company's stations were looking more like millstones than money machines.

168

Louis Kessler (right) and **Neil Brown** (third from right) started **KVOS** in Seattle in 1927, and moved the station to Bellingham after a few months. Brown built most of the equipment himself. Kessler managed the station. A great practical joker, Kessler sometimes donned fake "fright teeth" and tried to break up his own performers while they were on the air.

In this photo the ubiquitous "permanent ground" salesman (see p. 28) makes another sale.

Still, by mid-1930 Rogan and Harry Spence had gotten three of their stations barely into black ink. The exception was KPCB, which had something of a problem: nobody could hear the station! It was licensed for just 100 watts on 1500 kilocycles, a frequency so poor even the Federal Radio Commission inspectors complained they couldn't pick it up on their equipment ten blocks away.*

As Chet Huntley was later to phrase it, "the audience which never had heard of KPCB was tremendous."

Meanwhile Jones had dreamed up yet another venture, and had opened an office in Hollywood, where he was recording programs for syndication to small stations around the country. One was "The Adventures of Tom and Wash," a rather obvious imitation of "Amos 'n' Andy." "Tom" was Tom Breneman (so, for that matter, was "Wash") who would gain considerably more fame later on, as emcee of the "Breakfast in Hollywood" show on ABC.

Another show featured Breneman at the piano, playing and singing popular tunes of the day. Then there was something called "The Vagabond Baritone" and a program of chit-chat by "Bill Hatch" who was Rogan Jones himself.

The transcriptions were cut on thick sixteen-inch discs and to keep costs down, Jones bicycled them from station to station instead of making individual

---

* KPCB was on the ninth floor of the Shopping Tower (now the Insurance Center Building) at Third and Pine. The FRC offices and monitoring station were on the 21st floor of the Smith Tower, where Olmstead's KFQX had been.

KVOS studio on the mezzanine of the Hotel Henry, at State and Holly Streets, Bellingham, about 1928. At left is the usual announcer's desk with switches for cutting in performers' mikes. The window at right looked down into the hotel lobby.

pressings. There were constant complaints about breakage and poor sound quality. After a few heady weeks of seeming success, the cancellations started rolling in, and the project had to be abandoned.

Now the retrenching started. KPCB was reorganized as a new company, Queen City Broadcasting, and eventually sold to Saul Haas. Harry Spence dropped out of the partnership and took KXRO with him. KPQ, the Wenatchee station, was turned over to a manager whose instructions were not to spend a single dollar he could in any way avoid. Rogan Jones married a concert violinist, moved to Bellingham, and assumed the active management of KVOS.

Short, dapper Louis Kessler had first put KVOS on the air back in 1927 in Seattle. The 50-watt station was in the Rosita Villa apartment house on the western slope of Queen Anne Hill, and was supposed to be "Kessler's Voice Of Seattle."

But jovial Lou Kessler, who was Jewish, was more disposed to cracking good-natured ethnic jokes than to running an aggressive business. The station didn't do well. By year's end he decided to go where there was less competition and moved Seattle's "voice" some eighty miles northward to Bellingham.

Kessler renamed KVOS "The Mount Baker Station," signed up some local live talent, beefed up the station's power and tried this and that, but just couldn't seem to take in as much money as he was shelling out. Finally he went bust and creditors ran the station until Rogan Jones and Harry Spence came up from Aberdeen and took over.

Fred Goddard, who was Spence's brother-in-law, managed the station at first. He recalls one big advertiser in those days was W. Delbert Darst, self-styled "drugless physician" whose offices were across the street from KVOS. Darst put on nightly programs answering health questions sent in by listeners. His standard prescription for everything from colds to falling arches was one or more glasses of salty sauerkraut juice—a miraculous elixir which, oddly enough, could only be purchased at Darst's nearby establishment.

Other radio fare included a couple of high school kids who sang duets as "Oofty and Goofty," a mysterious Oriental clairvoyant named "Alla Tamanya," and a sad-eyed young lady who told people's fortunes from tea leaves.

The programming got a good deal livelier after Jones came on the scene.

170

Control room for **KVOS**, Bellingham, in 1930. The operator on duty is **H. Ben Murphy**. Note the telephones and switchboard, used to talk with the studio announcer and to place remote broadcasts on the air.

The Herald's Radio Department

COMPACT IS READY

International Radio Conference to Approve Program.

WASHINGTON, D. C., Nov. 25.—(AP)—The international radio conference was called together today to give its final approval to a new international wireless convention.

The compact will be the last word in efficient and scientific radio regulation, its drafters declare, combining elasticity for future improvements with elimination of past outstanding communication difficulties. The delegates of seventy-nine nations and territories assembled to pass in second and last reading on the new document which the conference has been busy negotiating since October 4. The ceremony of signing the treaty was next on the program.

Under terms of the convention the original of the treaty will be preserved in the state department here, where the exchange of ratifications also will take place.

The new convention's chief difference from the previous 1912 treaty and its peculiar importance arise principally from its allocation of wave lengths to the various international radio services and in the provisions for new radio activities whose possibilities were not even suspected in 1912.

Difference Slight

The bulk of the convention and of the regulations dealing with radio procedure, with rules for the operation of fixed and ship stations for distress and ordinary communications, and other routine cases, does not differ materially from the previous regulations.

Even one of the chief sources of satisfaction to the American delegation, namely, the principle which has been firmly established in this conference of maintaining all private operation of radio concerns free from governmental interference, is not strictly speaking in conflict with the provisions of the previous radio convention. However, in this parley, the American thesis had to withstand such serious pressure from European delegations that its retention is considered as a distinct success.

In allocation all wave lengths between 30,000 and five meters, the new convention amplifies the previous compact, as at that time short waves were entirely in the experimental stage.

POPULAR LOCAL RADIO STAR

PERDIN KORSMO

One of the favorite staff artists of KVOS, Bellingham's radio station, is Perdin Korsmo, tenor. While a resident here for some time, he came into prominence as a vocalist since KVOS was established Hallowe'en night and has been a "regular" ever since. Mr. Korsmo's accompanist is his wife, teacher of piano, and a talented pianist herself.

BATTLE BROADCAST

Notre Dame-Trojan Grid Game On Air Saturday.

(Special to The Herald)
SAN FRANCISCO, Nov. 25.—With interest running high in the intersectional football clash between the undefeated University of Southern California Trojans and the great Notre Dame university eleven of Southbend, Indiana, at Soldier Field, Chicago, Saturday, arrangements have been made by the National Broadcasting Company

THE HERALD RADIO DEPARTMENT

FRIDAY EVENING, NOV. 25.

KVOS (209.7) Bellingham: 4, radio dealers; 6, shopping tour; 7, studio program; 7:30, Aunt Helen's children's program; 8, studio program; 9, "Gloom Killers;" Fred and Gordon Richardson, vocalists; Maragret Drew, "blues" singer; Boerhave sisters, vocalists; Gordon Smith, steel guitar; Harry Ehlers, "uke" artist.

KFOA (447.5) Seattle: 5, Big Brothers' children's program; 6:45, Auto club bulletins; 7, concert orchestra; 8, Oldtime trio; 9, time signals; "An Hour In Memory Lane," from San Francisco; 10,

Rogan Jones was a shrewd, energetic businessman with a zest for challenges. His prime goal was not just to make money—though he acknowledged money was a mighty good measure of success! (Once, when KVOS moved to a new building, he insisted on standing directly under the company's safe as it was hoisted several stories up. "If anything happens to the money, there's no use my sticking around!" he quipped.)

And he had principles. There was that time in Aberdeen he took a strong editorial stand against the power company, even though they were his biggest advertiser and he was liable to lose their business—which he did.

What Rogan had most was an almost visionary urge to pioneer. His great joy was in proving a worthwhile thing could be done, even against great odds—which generally meant a serious lack of capital. He called that "shoestringing." Just about all Rogan's business life was spent "shoestringing." He preferred to keep his brains busy and his checkbook idle.

Now Rogan's challenge in those Depression years was to find a cheap way for KVOS to hit an apathetic community between the eyes and get its avid attention. What he came up with got the heed of not just Bellingham but two great industries, several judges, the national press and, finally, the United States Supreme Court.

Ever since radio's beginnings there had been some broadcasting of news on most stations. And quite commonly this involved "lifting" selected items from local papers and reading them on the air, with or without permission of the newspapers in question. Often enough, it was merely a matter of summarizing the day's headlines; or maybe quoting lead paragraphs from a few top stories. "Newscasts" didn't make much splash in the average station's schedule.

Rogan decided that was all wrong. Beginning in 1933 he set aside time for three big daily news shows: thirty minutes each in the morning and at noon, and a whopping three quarters of an hour evenings. The exact times were determined after careful study of the press schedules for the Bellingham Herald's two daily editions, as well as the train and bus schedules from Seattle.

The programs were called "Newspaper of the Air," and were unabashed readings of all the principal stories from the Bellingham Herald, the Seattle Times, and the Seattle P-I. And there was nothing coy about the program format. "We give you the news before you can buy it," trumpeted the newscaster, who went on to imply there really was no need for his listeners to *buy* a newspaper at all any more!

Understandably this new KVOS "service," as it was billed, was greeted with something approaching apoplexy in business offices of the newspapers, but

Leslie Harrison Darwin, controversial newscaster on **KVOS** in the 1930s, brought the United States press-radio "war" to a climax. Newspaper-owned press associations were refusing service to broadcasters, so Darwin pirated material from columns of the Bellingham Herald and the Seattle Times and P-I. The resulting legal challenge went all the way to the U.S. Supreme Court.

especially the Herald, which threatened Rogan with legal action if he didn't knock off the piracy.

Ironically, the Herald Company itself had twice been involved in broadcasting in Bellingham and had twice given up the field. From 1922 to 1924 they operated KDZR, a small 50-watt station on the second floor of their triangular newspaper plant. They abandoned that, and later gave away the transmitter to a KVOS engineer, who built a ham rig with part of it.

And when Lou Kessler went broke with KVOS, Herald publisher Frank Ira Sefrit was one of the big creditors. He subsequently sold his interest—to Rogan Jones.

But what really frosted Sefrit was that Rogan had cannily hired as his newscaster a crusty white-haired Democratic ex-newspaper executive who happened to be Sefrit's bitterest enemy. He was Leslie H. Darwin, who until 1912 had been editor of the Herald's mortal competitor, the Reveille and American. Darwin was always railing editorially against big business, Republican politicians, and the ultra-conservative Bellingham Herald, which of course railed right back. Finally Big Business bought Darwin's paper and fired him, and gave his job to Sefrit.

The two men never forgave each other.

Darwin came back to Bellingham in 1922 and

←
The Bellingham Herald's "Radio Department" shared space with patent medicine ads back in 1927. **KVOS** was in the bloom of its first weeks' operation at the time; before long the Herald would be attacking KVOS, rather than promoting it.

started a new paper, the American, with which to resume his vitriolic crusade. In 1929 he sold out, and part of the deal was his pledge to stay out of journalism in Bellingham for five years.

Yet here he was again some three years later, not only broadcasting for free the stories Sefrit had to pay his reporters to write, but larding his programs with less-than-subtle jibes at his ancient foe, Frank Sefrit.

"This will make the wildcat wilder!" Darwin would howl in his shrieking, near-soprano voice as he reported, say, Franklin Roosevelt's latest program to aid labor unions.

Sefrit replied in kind. Frequent editorials blasted away at Darwin in language that left readers goggle-eyed. The announcer was referred to (among other things) as "the local radio outlaw," "a hop head," "braying moron," "mental sot," "a common liar," "brazen upstart," "professional trouble maker," "the radio howler," a "conscienceless rascal," etc. etc. etc.

When name-calling didn't shut Darwin up, Sefrit decided the thing to do was to start a competing radio station. He applied for a license, but Rogan went to the FCC with clippings out of Sefrit's own paper to show the whole purpose of it was just to put KVOS out of business. "Not in the public interest," said Roosevelt's men on the FCC, and ruled in favor of Rogan, a lifelong Democrat.

Meanwhile alarmed newspaper publishers across the land were clamoring for action against broadcasters' brazen trespassing on the Fourth Estate. (Otherwise, warned one association president, "newspapers will be nothing but a memory on a tablet at Radio City!")

It was the Associated Press which finally brought suit against KVOS, on behalf of the Herald, the P-I, and the Times.* Not for infringement of the copyright laws—those laws didn't yet extend to the broadcasting of hard news—but for "unfair competition."

KVOS's attorneys included no less a legal light than United States Senator Clarence C. Dill. Dill just happened to be the man who wrote the government's brand new regulatory "bible," the Communications Act of 1934. By broadcasting the news, he argued now, KVOS was merely fulfilling its legally mandated obligation to be of public service.

Judge John Bowen agreed. Once news reports are "published and distributed to the public," Brown held, they "from that moment belong to the public." And KVOS was part of "the public"!

Brown's ruling horrified publishers everywhere. Many lashed back editorially. "Who Owns the News?" whined the prestigious "Literary Digest." "Specious... amazing...astonishing," groaned "Editor & Publisher." "A Fight to the Last Adjective," promised "News-Week."

The Supreme Court penned that final adjective the following year, at the end of the appeals trail. Judge Bowen was sustained on a technicality. And radio's

right to air the news has never come in question again since.

So the Great News War ended at last. One by one the press associations opened their memberships to radio stations. Most of these (and KVOS stood first in line) quite gladly installed the teletype machines that were proffered them, and paid to be fed more news each day than they could possibly use.

Like most pioneer-spirited broadcasters, Rogan Jones looked forward to the coming of television with an eagerness matched only by his dismay at learning what a station would cost to build and operate. KRSC-TV spent a third of a million getting on the air, and people who knew assured him it couldn't be done for less.

But Rogan wasn't so sure. A lifetime of "shoe-stringing" had convinced him there was always a way to cut costs a little more, a little more. As the government freeze on applications went into effect, he accepted the breathing space, and mapped out a plan.

Channel 5 didn't come in well in Bellingham, so there weren't many sets there yet. Rogan figured he'd better make sure of an audience *before* he spent money building a station, and he began looking for ways to beef up 5's signal locally. At that time there was a fellow in Astoria, Oregon experimenting with something called a community antenna system, and Rogan sent his engineers down to have a look.

Ed Parsons had about 200 sets on his primitive cable system, but he had a good many technical problems, too. Rogan's chief engineer, Ernie Harper, looked the system over and concluded it could be made to work well. He picked Parsons' brains and bought some of Parsons' gear, went back to Bellingham and built up some equipment from scratch.

Meanwhile salesmen were signing up the first hundred customers. Coaxial cable was strung from subscriber to subscriber, using poles, trees, garages and whatever else came in handy.

And it worked! Soon KVOS TV-Cable was signing up new set owners by the hundreds. It was, by one way of figuring, the first really successful system in the country. (The Parsons cable and one in Pottsville, Pa. were operating earlier, but not all that well, according to KVOS's manager at the time, Jack Clarke.) Then in 1951 the FCC published its proposed allocations of TV channels—and no VHF channel was to be assigned to Bellingham! Two UHF slots were listed for the town, but that was small help, since virtually no TV sets were being manufactured to get UHF as yet. Even the FCC must have figured Bellingham was too small for a "real" TV station.

There was a curious thing, though. Channel 12, a VHF frequency, was earmarked for Chilliwack, just across the border in British Columbia. And Chilliwack is less than half the size of Bellingham.

So Rogan petitioned the FCC for a rules change

---

* Oddly enough, Darwin was a brother-in-law of Seattle Times publisher Alden Blethen.

174

Channel 12 doing a remote telecast of the annual Blossom Time festival in Bellingham, about 1955, when the station finally acquired some live TV cameras.

giving channel 12 to Bellingham instead. Of course this depended on Canada's ceding the channel to the United States, which—after some months of hearings and international horse-trading—it agreed to do.

At length KVOS got its permit to put in a transmitter. Trouble was, Rogan didn't have money to go out and buy one; so his engineers began constructing their own. The visual (picture) side was built at KPQ, the Wenatchee station, using old radio transmitter cabinets and as many scrounged parts as possible. The aural (sound) side was built up in Bellingham from a used FM radio transmitter. KVOS was thus one of just two or three stations in the country to use largely home-made transmitting gear.

Meanwhile an interesting question was raised at a meeting of Rogan's top staffers. The station would probably put a fair signal into Vancouver, B.C. Should they accept advertising by Canadians, if it were offered them?

Rogan was dubious. He wasn't really anxious to court Canadian business. His burning design was to make small-town American television feasible, and he

was counting on local U.S. merchants to be the operation's mainstay. Still, he decided, Canadian ads would not be turned away, either.

So when KVOS-TV hit the air on June 3, 1952 it was "Your Peace Arch Station, serving Northwest Washington and British Columbia." And the inaugural program was a BBC kinescope of the coronation of Queen Elizabeth.

(Western Canada had no stations on the air yet, so the British government flew the films out to Rogan from London. They landed in Vancouver hours late, and the Royal Canadian Mounted Police escorted them to the border, where the Washington State Patrol took over and sped them to Bellingham for airing.)

KVOS-TV in its first year was a bare-bones operation if ever there was one. The station hadn't a single TV camera; it could only show films and slides. There was no sports coverage. Local news was simply read "voice over" a slide. There was no network hookup. Once in a great while, special programs (such as the World Series) were picked up from Seattle on a TV set and rebroadcast.

Rogan Jones (left), founder of **KVOS-TV**, with Public Affairs Director **Hoyt Wertz** and "Around the World Press Conference" contest winner **Sharon Drysdale** in 1958. Sharon was judged the best questioner on a panel of youngsters who interviewed foreign college students.

Jones, who ran the station on a shoestring, liked to think up programs like this that cost next to nothing to produce.

The station only operated in the evening. Even so, there were long interruptions when the equipment failed. And when it didn't, the pictures came in weak, and engineers feared to run more power lest the home-made transmitting antenna burn up.

Ads were sparse. Creditors were grumbling. Rogan's financial resources were running out fast, and broadcasters the length of Puget Sound looked for the station to fold at any time.

Meanwhile Rogan was receiving contingents of British Columbia advertising executives who kept assuring him of the very solid need for commercial television in B.C. The big problem was Channel 12's picture: it was ghosty and variable in Vancouver, and Victoria couldn't get it at all. They urged Rogan again and again to improve his Canadian coverage by beefing up his signal in that direction.

One day at a company picnic, Rogan and Ernie Harper were strolling along the beach, chatting. They kept looking across the salt chuck toward the conspicuous hump of half-mile-high Mount Constitution, on Orcas Island, and both were thinking the same thing. "There," Harper said at last, "is where we ought to put our station. Why we'd get a clear shot at the whole area, including Vancouver and Victoria."

Indeed, the summit of Mount Constitution commands, Gibraltar-like, the most populous areas of B.C. and northwestern Washington State. It happens also to be part of a State-owned park. Rogan got busy and made a deal with the Parks and Recreation Commission to lease space for a couple of small buildings and an antenna tower.

KVOS also negotiated with the General Electric Company for a reconditioned TV transmitter on long-term credit. It was loaded on board a Washington State ferry and moved to Orcas Island over a weekend in 1954. A small crew of engineers was hired to ride herd on it and keep the station's voracious diesel electric generator fueled, since the mountain top lacked commercial power at that time. (The technicians were obliged to buy jeeps in order to negotiate the twisting, timbered mountain road to work each day, summer and winter. The prudent ones kept snowshoes, shovels and axes handy, too.)

There was no telephone line to the transmitter site. The only communication was with the studio in Bellingham, over surplus World War Two tank radios —when they could be made to work.

But little by little, the miracle took place. KVOS signed a contract with CBS. (Programs were simply

KVOS-TV's rustic transmitter building on the summit of Mount Constitution in Moran State Park, Orcas Island, about 1958. The antenna tower, fed by underground transmission lines, is out of the photo to the left. Cabin in foreground was used by state fire watchers during the summer months.

picked up off-the-air from Channel 11, in Tacoma.) Business picked up, too, especially in Canada, even after the Canadian channels came on the air: most viewers preferred watching American programs. And gradually, the old, primitive and second-hand equipment was replaced with dependable, higher-power gear.

The principal author of the miracle was a bright, personable young executive named Dave Mintz. Mintz was just out of college when he saw an ad in "Broadcasting" Magazine, placed by Rogan Jones, who wanted a new radio station manager. That was back in 1947. Rogan specified five years' experience was needed, and Mintz didn't have that, but he clipped out the ad and saved it. Five years later he wrote Rogan a letter, enclosing the old ad and saying he now had the experience and so could he have the job, please?

Impressed, Rogan wrote back and said "yes."

Actually Jones was notorious for changing managers frequently. Sometimes he went through five or six a year. Most simply couldn't keep up with Rogan, who was an absolute idea machine, except that Tuesday's idea was often the exact opposite of Monday's. And he was not a man to be disagreed with.

Dave Mintz perceived that Rogan's dream of "shoe-stringing" a small-town TV station to solvency just wasn't going to work. To serve Bellingham viably, KVOS-TV would have to serve British Columbia, too. Mintz became executive vice-president in 1953, and promptly embarked on a parlous strategy: to steer KVOS-TV on a persistent course toward the maximum possible business—wherever it came from—while coping as diplomatically as possible with the stream of conflicting and time-consuming ideas that kept pouring from Rogan's fertile brain.

Mintz's course was a success. So much so that the station was into the black in a few short years. But only *after* KVOS-TV came so near foundering that he and Ernie Harper mortgaged their homes, cars, and insurance policies to buy into the company and keep it afloat.

By 1961, KVOS-TV was a prosperous, well run and solidly financed business with a bright long-term future. It was sold then to a Florida-based corporation, Wometco Enterprises, Inc.,* for enough millions of dollars to guarantee Rogan's next venture wouldn't have to "shoestring" at all.

---

* Coincidentally, Wometco also owns WTVJ in Miami, at the southeasternmost edge of the nation, while KVOS is the continental U.S.A.'s northwesternmost station.

And that next venture was already launched. After an unsuccessful effort to get the television franchise for all of Nigeria (a change in African politics squelched the deal at the last minute) Rogan went on a trip, visiting some broadcasting stations in the Soviet Union along the way. He found them operating by automatic equipment. Impressed, he concluded that automation was broadcasting's wave of the future. He also concurred with Ernie Harper's idea that FM radio was going to come into its own, finally. Always the visionary, Rogan melded these two notions into a pioneering scheme that was big, and theoretical, and years ahead of its time.

Rogan was no fan of rock-and-roll. Even in the early fifties he had circulated a memo describing modern pop music as "cacophonous, neurotic...instrumentalized hysteria" and "musical epilepsy," and banning from his stations all "be-bop, hot jazz or whatever terms apply to wailing reeds and screaming brasses." He decided that what FM listeners needed now was a good dose of Bach, Brahms, and Beethoven.

Along with that, Rogan revived the old, failed vision of his Hollywood days: the mass production of low-cost programming for small radio stations. He decided to market not just the equipment, or "hardware," for automation but the tape recorded program material (the "software") to go with it.

R. H. "Andy" Anderson, scarcely out of school, became operations director for **KVOS-TV**, Bellingham, in 1958.

Al Swift, the future U.S. congressman, working his way through Central Washington State College as a full-time announcer for **KXLE**, Ellensburg, about 1956.

Swift later became news and public affairs director for **KVOS-TV**, Bellingham. Turning to politics, he was elected Washington's Second Congressional District representative in 1978.

General Manager **Dave Mintz** (right) and Public Affairs Director **Al Swift** display one of the station's numerous awards for locally produced public affairs programming.

Popular Bellingham broadcaster **Haines Fay** (left) being presented with symbolic "20-year contract" on completing two decades with Rogan Jones' stations, in 1966. The radio station call had been changed to **KGMI**, following sale of KVOS-TV to a Miami company.

Fay was a high-school sports reporter and PA announcer when Jones first heard him. Invited to do a play-by-play broadcast of a football game, he did so well Jones hired him forthwith. With time out to finish school and do a hitch in the Navy, he's been with the station ever since.

With Fay are Station Manager **Jim Hamstreet**, announcer **Bob Concie**, and **Jones**.

Jim French was one of the first DJ's to record music lead-ins for automated music stations. Before that, French—one of the readiest wits in the business—was the popular emcee of a long-running morning program on **KIRO**.

It was French who, along with equally zany Al Cummings, spoofed listeners with the "hypnotically induced" recall of Cummings' "earlier life" as a Civil War rebel. The supposed experiments, in the wake of the Bridey Murphy reincarnation furor, ended abruptly when some religious and spiritualist groups began taking the gag seriously.

Other hoaxes of that era included sighting of the horrible Lake Union sea serpent, and plans to build a lead balloon factory in downtown Seattle.

Jones hired Alfred Wallenstein, the famous symphony conductor, to head up the new program service. He hired cultured-sounding, multi-linguistic announcers, and a building full of engineers to design and build equipment. He put KGMI, an FM station, on the air in Bellingham as a pilot operation, to test everything. Then (in partnership with Dave Mintz and Ernie Harper) he bought more FM stations: KGMJ in Seattle, KGMB in Portland, KBAY in San Francisco, KFMU in Los Angeles, KFMW in San Bernardino.

None of the stations made money. Inside of a few years Rogan was selling them off again, one by one.

For one thing, it was too early for FM. There just weren't enough receiving sets in existence. And then, the bugs hadn't all been worked out of the new automatic gear.

Program tapes were loaded in huge reels onto twin

playback machines, with commercials and station breaks standing by on a third apparatus. Sub-audible tones on the tapes were supposed to switch the machines on and off at appropriate times. But all too often the switching came *in*appropriately instead—in the midst of some crashing symphonic climax, say, or halfway through a vigorous violin cadenza, which triggered the tape change.

Or the commercial tape would get stuck and play sixteen station identifications in a row.

Or the whole operation would stop dead and nobody would even notice.

Such problems were solvable, of course. Indeed, Rogan's pioneer company—International Good Music Inc.—is a leading manufacturer of automation today, with hundreds of dependable systems in service around North America.

What wasn't solvable was the modern listener's new taste in music. Forty years before, when men like Rogan Jones and Vincent Kraft saw their first microphones, radio couldn't really handle "good" music. Transmitters and receivers lacked fidelity. So did recordings. Live performances cost too much.

So radio helped popularize a cheaper, less demanding kind of music.

By the time of these pioneers' passing (Kraft in 1971, Jones in '72) FM radio offered sparkling clean stereo sound, hi-fi speakers were fixtures in many homes, tape and disc recordings were indistinguishable from live broadcasts.

Never since the dawning of time had such treasures of music been so casually and universally available.

But few old "radiophans" still yearned for Bach and Brahms. What really turned them on in the seventies was, man, like, I mean, the screaming distorted brasses and wailing amplified reeds of Rogan's despised "musical epilepsy."

→

TV in the courtroom. In a memorable moment, confessed "Hillside Strangler" **Kenneth Bianchi** breaks down during guilty plea as Channel 12's **Andy Anderson** watches on nearby monitor. Modern lightweight gear called ENG (for **E**lectronic **N**ews **G**athering) provides for faster, less obtrusive news coverage than ever before.

For this 1979 hearing, **KVOS-TV** provided pool video and audio to Seattle stations and the national networks.

KVOS-TV News Director **"Andy" Anderson** (right) with co-anchor **Mary Starrett** and the station's unconventional weather-man, **Dr. Charles "Jerry" Flora**. Flora is a marine biologist and former president of Western Washington University.

The talented trio's "10:30 Report" was KVOS-TV's first live local news show in the station's 27-year history. The nightly program debuted in 1979.

CHAPTER TWELVE

Stay Tuned for Tomorrow

Trying to guess the future can be risky—as the Rogan Joneses of every era can assure you.

We need no crystal ball, though, to glimpse with fair clarity what broadcasting's next decades could be like. Broadcasting is after all a kind of magic, and ever depends on the state of its technological art. Today's laboratory wizards largely determine what tomorrow's public will see and hear.

One revolutionary development already above the horizon—literally—is the communications satellite. Suspended in permanent orbit some 22,000 miles over the equator, it beams television programs to TV stations, to cable companies, even to individual homes in such isolated regions as Alaska's great hinterland.

Or rather *they* do, because at this writing there are eleven North American satellites in place already, with a total capacity of more than fifty different channels. And more are coming.

With satellites, more and more people will have access to more and more choices of programming. If you don't care for what six or eight local stations are offering, just keep spinning your dials. *Something* will appeal to you, whether it's a first-run movie from L. A., bull fights from Mexico, or the Follies, direct from gay Paree.

Even more revolutionary, say the electronics wise guys, is something called OF. That stands for optical fibers, which are fine glass threads, thin as human hairs. They can transmit radio and TV signals in the form of light impulses, the way old-fashioned wires transmit electricity, but many times more efficiently.

With OF there's no static, no distortion, no interference from the CB set down the street. More to the point, a smallish cable like the one on your telephone could hold a bundle of optical fibers capable of transmitting to your home *billions* of phone calls, TV programs, computer printouts, video games, stock market reports, news and weather summaries, bank and store transactions, University extension courses, medical diagnoses, live or recorded concerts and plays, newspapers, and best-selling books, all at the same time. You just have to dial up the one you want, much as you dial phone calls today.

TV sets will (at long last) have crystal-clear stereophonic sound, with auxiliary channels to punch up in case you prefer to watch "Three's Company" in Spanish or French.

Tomorrow's counterpart of home movies will be home TV. "Shoot" the kids with a tiny wireless camera, record the results on your own video-tape cassette, and play it back as often as you like.

Video discs will be as common as LP records. You'll play them through your TV set, on a laser-equipped turntable, to watch favorite movies and plays again and again.

With all this competition, individual broadcast stations and networks will have to settle for audiences rather less "broad" than in the past. The word for tomorrow may well be "narrowcasting." That is, there should be more programming, finally, for smaller interest groups. And less frenetic scrambling to gain mass audiences for every single show.

TV networks, like the old radio nets before them, may give up broadcasting entertainment altogether and concentrate on covering news and special events. Local stations will go independent so they can pick and choose from the offerings of movie companies and other private producers of TV fare.

There will be decreasing government regulation of over-the-air broadcasting. The old fear that a few companies might monopolize the public airwaves will give way before the billion-channel capability of modern technology.

Broadcasting won't be as chancy—nor as much fun—as it once was. Automated, computer-like equipment will replace the button-pushers and knob-twirlers in control rooms everywhere. Virtually everything on the air will be pre-recorded, pre-edited, pre-tested, slickly packaged and essentially untouched by human hands. Gone will be the days of "bloopers," of announcers breaking up with laughter, of horseplay behind the scenes, of sound effects that don't work, records getting stuck, slides upside down, films running out too soon, transmitters blowing up, microphones and cameras going dead—or staying "live" too long!

On the other hand, with cable hookups as commonplace as the family telephone in tomorrow's wired cities, there's no reason why a multitude of small, community-type TV studios can't make their offerings available to any homes that care to tune them in. Everything from school concerts and PTA meetings to little theater productions and precinct political rallies could be covered by neighborhood TV entrepreneurs.

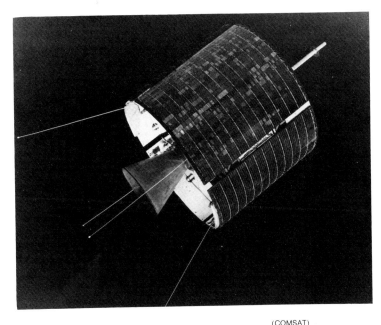

(COMSAT)

"Live via satellite!" The world's first geosynchronous commercial communications satellite, nicknamed "Early Bird," went into orbit over the Atlantic in 1965. For the first time in history, U.S. networks could transmit TV shows direct from Europe. Today, such originations are commonplace.

An earth satellite station for direct reception of TV signals from anywhere in North America. This installation at **KSTW** in Tacoma was the first of its kind in the Puget Sound country. A considerable portion of KSTW's daily schedule is by satellite. The former **KTNT-TV**, now owned by Oklahoma-based Gaylord Broadcasting Co., also has ultra-modern studios in Tacoma and new transmitting facilities on Seattle's Capital Hill.

The new look of broadcasting. Automatic equipment for radio stations can do just about everything these days but sweep out the studio.

In this "Basic A" system manufactured by IGM of Bellingham, computers switch automatically between prerecorded entertainment and announcement tapes, including musical selections, "canned" disc jockey chatter, station identifications, commercials and even time signals.

Automation can also switch in and out of network on cue, keep a printed log of operations, handle billing for advertisers. Human beings only need take over for news flashes, sportscasts, and interviews.

TV-like monitor screen (at left) shows station personnel what the machines are up to from minute to minute.

Two-way satellite TV will some day bring state-of-the-art health services to every corner of the shrinking globe, as "broadcasting" expands to new roles. In this recent University of Washington experiment, Indian Health Service physicians at Fort Yukon, Alaska, conferred with big-city specialists on the diagnosis and treatment of patients. Satellite pictures were clearer, with better color and less interference, than home TV reception.

Note satellite dish antennas at right, aimed almost parallel to the ground. At the Arctic Circle, equatorial satellites lie barely over the horizon.

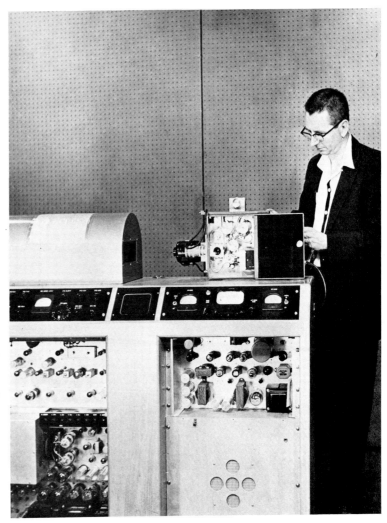

Before tape recording was adapted to TV, programs were "recorded" on film by this sort of rig, called a "kinescope recorder." It amounted to making a movie by aiming a film camera at a small-screen TV monitor. Here **KCTS** Chief Engineer **John Boor** fiddles with a recorder built specially for Channel 9 in the 50's.

By contrast, today's TV news photographer records his shots on a portable tape machine slung over a shoulder. The size: not much larger than a bread box.

Starting up a small television outlet could become as casual a thing as launching a neighborhood newspaper. All you would need would be a couple of cameras, a microphone or two, and a spare room fitted out with a table and chairs and perhaps some plush looking drapes on the wall. A piano would be nice to have, and if your neighbor boy plays the violin....

So broadcasting on Puget Sound could well come full circle. What started in the garages and basements of the Vincent Krafts and Palmer Lebermans, to become the empires of Saul Haases and O. D. Fishers, having circled the earth and prowled the moon and sent us pictures of planets, having amazed us and thrilled, entertained, educated and, yes, sometimes bored us to tears—broadcasting will come home again.

And then perhaps the magic window will not open on the extraordinary and momentous things of the world and the cosmos only. It may get around at last to showing us also those smaller, homelier, but equally precious wonders of our own community, our backyards, and ourselves.

End of the disc jockey era. For a quarter century, **Al Cummings** was dean of Puget Sound radio's madcap, super-personality DJ's. In this recent photo, Al makes a last broadcast over **KXA**.

APPENDIX

For History Buffs...

To say which broadcasting station was "first" in the Puget Sound country is impossible in the absence of universally accepted criteria as to what, in fact, constituted a "broadcasting station" in the earliest days. The federal government did not begin regularly licensing radio stations for broadcasts to the public until September, 1921. By that time, any number of radio "hams"—some licensed and some not—had long been attracting listeners with experimental transmissions of music and other forms of entertainment.

Two newspaper-owned stations, KFC (the Seattle P-I) and KGB (the Tacoma Ledger) were licensed on December 8, 1921. They were the first U.S. stations west of Chicago and north of Stockton, California to be formally authorized for the broadcast service.

Of these, it seems KGB did not actually get a signal on the air until early in 1922.

KFC, on the other hand, had *already* been in operation as a broadcasting station since early July of 1921. Possibly they used an amateur or experimental call sign and license, but no documentation of this has been found. The P-I's own columns at the time made no mention of call letters.

Predating KFC's initial programs by some months were intermittent voice and music broadcasts of Vincent Kraft, over his ham station, 7XC. The transmissions originated from the garage of Kraft's home on 19th Avenue N.E. On March 14, 1922, his broadcasting activity was formalized by the assignment of a government license and the call letters KJR.

KJR is thus one of two stations, still on the air in Seattle, which have claimed the distinction of being the area's "first" radio station. Its rival for this honor is KTW, founded by the well-known City Light president and engineer, James Delmage Ross, and installed under the domes of the old First Presbyterian Church building in 1922. It was licensed April 14 of that year, and began regular weekly (Sundays only) religious programming on May 14.

The church's own records, however, indicate some trial broadcasts had been made there as far back as August 20, 1920. No further documentation of this claim has been discovered, and Ross' nephew recalls hearing that the earlier experiments were not very successful. The equipment only put out a few watts' power, and most of that never made it to the antenna, but was radiated uselessly inside the church's cavernous building. The station was unlicensed, and its audience—if any—limited to a few nearby neighbors.

Certainly many radio buffs were tinkering with 'phone transmission in 1920, some of whom ultimately built broadcasting stations. They include, for example, the Leese brothers of Everett, who later founded KFBL (now KRKO); and Father Sebastian Ruth of St. Martin's College, at Lacey, whose 7YS (now KGY), licensed even earlier than the Kraft station, may in truth be the region's "first" radio voice.

For Nostalgia Fans...

(A note: This section is included as a service to interested readers. Nothing is to be construed as an endorsement. The information is believed correct as of the date of publication, but in common with all matters of human endeavor, is liable to change at any time.)

A renewed fascination for "old time radio" has been sweeping the country in recent years. Actual broadcasts of programs ranging from "The Lone Ranger" to "You Bet Your Life" can be purchased in many record stores. Tapes, LP's and cassettes are sold by numerous mail order companies, including one called simply "Nostalgia" at P.O. Box 82, Redmond, WA 98052. This company handles the SPOKANE, TOTEM, RADIO ARCHIVES and AIR-CHECK labels which feature old shows by Bing Crosby, Rudy Vallee, Ruth Etting, Dennis Day, Mel Torme, and many others.

Or, you can still laugh along with Stan Boreson's Scandihoovian dialect songs and parodies (like "Walking in My Winter Underwear," and "The Waitress at Norway Hall"). A good selection of Stan's recordings is available at the Ballard Record Shop, 5512 20th Avenue N.W., Seattle 98107. Doug Setterberg, who often appeared with Stan on TV, is featured on a number of albums such as the hilarious "Yust Try to Sing Along in Swedish with Doug Setterberg & Stan Boreson."

Doug Setterberg (left) and **Stan Boreson** doing one of their popular Norwegian song parodies.

And a memorial recording of Leo Lassen broadcast excerpts has been produced by sportscaster Wayne Cody. Titled "The Leo Lassen Story" the disc includes retrospective interviews with newspaper and sports figures who knew Seattle's famous baseball announcer. It costs $6.95 plus tax by mail from the American Productions Co., 3428 25th Avenue W. #301, Seattle 98199.

Serious collectors of old radio programs store them by the hundreds—or thousands—on reel-to-reel tapes they make up themselves. By using 1800-foot tapes and slow recording speeds, six or even twelve hours of programming will fit on each reel. (This involves the use of stereo equipment, with separate programs being recorded on left and right tracks in both directions.) Most collectors use two machines, with patch cords for copying or "dubbing" from one machine to the other. Duplicated tapes may be easily traded with other aficionados; thus one builds as large a collection as desired.

To get started, new collectors can rent tapes of old time radio shows for a modest fee. For information write Len Lawson, 1206 Notre Dame Ct., Livermore, CA 94550.

Trading partners are readily located through the pages of various publications devoted to the hobby. One of the most useful is a monthly mimeographed newsletter called "Hello Again," published by Jay Hickerson, Box C, Orange, CT 06477.

One of the most complete archives of vintage radio programs in existence is the Milo Ryan Phonoarchive of the University of Washington's School of Communications, Seattle, WA 98195. Thousands of radio shows are included in the collection, which began with a gift from KIRO of some 2500 old instantaneous transcription discs dating to 1939 and after. KOMO and CBS have donated more material to the archive, which has been further augmented from a variety of sources.

Sound quality of the University's recordings is generally quite good. Even the networks have sometimes obtained copies of their own past shows from the Phonoarchive, in making up those retrospective salutes to radio that are aired on various occasions.

Material in the Milo Ryan Phonoarchive is not available to the casual hobbyist, but educators engaged in serious research work can make arrangements to get copies of programs they need. Contact the curator, Professor Donald Godfrey.

Another popular pastime is restoring old radio and TV sets to their original condition. "Vintage Radio," Box 2045, Palos Verdes Peninsula, CA 90274 is a leading source of information. Locally, if you're nostalgic for the days when radios came in fine wood cabinets, or an even earlier era when "radio" meant sparks crashing about the contacts of a Morse operator's key, there are two groups of kindred souls. Try the Antique Wireless Association, in care of Warren Green, 7202 N. Mercer Way, Mercer Island, WA 98040. Or contact John Keene, president of the Puget Sound Wireless Association, at 2634 Ellis Street, Bellingham, WA 98225.

Fan clubs still unite the devotees of old radio shows and performers. One of the most interesting is the "Friends of Vic and Sade" who keep green the memory of Paul Rhymer's uniquely delicious comedy. Periodic newsletters abound with remembered trivia surrounding the immortal Gook family and their myriad associates, like Mr. Gumpox the garbage man, "Smelly" Clark and Bluetooth Johnson, Chuck and Dottie Brainfeeble, Miz Razerscum, and the ever-popular Rishigan Fishigan, from Sishigan, Michigan. If you're into V & S, write Barbara Schwarz, 7232 N. Keystone Avenue, Lincolnwood, Ill. 60646.

For Poetry Lovers...

Surely few baseball fans ever suspected that Leo Lassen, Seattle's famous sportscaster, was also the author of a great deal of insightful and sensitive poetry. His work was rarely published, except at Christmas time, when for many years Leo would have a small folder of verses printed and, bound with ribbons, sent out to a small circle of friends and associates. Here is a sampling of those holiday offerings by the legendary "Mr. Baseball."

WHO KNOWS?
(For Dorothy Rippe)

Who knows in some fled yesterday
   But that you were fair Guinevere,
And I of Arthur's Table Round,
   Forgetting vows while you were near?

Who knows but that you might have been
   The Juliet of that balcony
Who pledged her heart one summer's night
   To Romeo—and I was he?

Who knows but that when Greece was young,
   Eurydice, with the simple strain
Of Orpheus' lyre I lured you back
   From death itself to life again?

But yesterdays are forgotten now,
   Today you are but Dorothy,
Far more concerned with dolls and things
   And gladly leave these thoughts to me.

WISDOM
(For Kenneth Bradley)

You think me wise, because my years are more,
And you are young and still an April lad,
The while you teach me wisdom I once had—
To take but what each moment has in store.
Aye, what is wisdom? Is it only lore
Of histories long dead to vaguely clad
A prophecy? Or is it to make glad
A way so many feet have walked before?

Ah, youth is more than just an interlude!
And age is measured not by sands that spill;
For I have learned that each is but a mood,
And man is young or old as he may will.
The songs of youth are silver trumpets blown,
And only age hears discord in their tone!

ADMONITION

The farther field is the fairer field,
   The greener field and gay!
And youth must learn what it will yield,
   O, tarry not a day!

And should you know what they will find
   And frown if they explore,
Perhaps you have the wiser mind,
   But you are young no more!

THE BRIMMING CUP

"My cup runneth over."
—Psalms, 23:5

I

This much is mine, when all is said and done:
A knowledge of my days, comprised, in brief,
Of memories, collected, one by one,
From remnants of endeavor and belief.
From time to time I find it well to take
An inventory, sorting odds and ends
of this remembered store and then to make
A budget for some sacrifice for friends.

Possession, at its best, maintains a hold
Of doubtful strength on what we build or buy;
And even thoughts that we would have untold
We never own, no matter how we try.
I learned of this from living, day by day:
That all we keep is what we give away.

II

And, too, from such experience, I learned
A truth which had been proved so long before:
That none but you is very much concerned
With old complaints of trouble you once bore.
And to this charge I plead that I have been
As guilty as the next; it could not last.
There is too much undone, too much unseen,
To stay in tangled traffic with the past.

While laughter is employed as many things—
A darting sword, a shield, a vague disguise—
When it should be no more than bubbling springs
For mirth that's quick with joy, it still supplies
A valued decoration; I believe
A burnished heart can ornament a sleeve.

III

I speak of knowledge, knowing it's confined
Within this narrow corner and that I
Have had no ready chance to free my mind
Of these familiar scenes, this bit of sky.
The most of us are better qualified
For one horizon and its small affairs;
But surely all of wit is not allied
With grave events that distance only shares.

Reality is bordered by the dreams
Of recollection and a new desire;
It is the present that too often seems
Disturbed by what we had or may acquire.
And they who always seek a farther star
May never find the heaven where they are.

IV

That I be understood, I have no aim
To recommend a creed or prophecy;
As shadows must be servile to a flame,
So we are bound to frayed philosophy.
Another truth of which I've come to know
Is I accomplish just so much alone;
And my rewards are few unless I show
A heed for welfare other than my own.

Ambition is the sharpest spur for pride;
It runs away without the check of reins.
To strive for its own sake is justified,
But service should be mingled with the gains.
A laurel wreath soon withered is success
Which has been stripped from vanquished happiness.

V

Of disappointments I have had a deal,
With profit from them as I plan ahead;
It turns to loss whenever I reveal
A bitterness I should have left unsaid.
I make mistakes and utilize them, too;
The cloudy days add pleasure to the fair.
My chief regard is that I cede my due
Within the bounds of my allotted square.

Contentment is not measured by the ease
Of mere existence; that serene estate
Is founded on those efforts made to please
And must be fostered to accumulate.
Because we have such need of one another
We join our doorways ever to each other.

VI

As I admit, whatever I might know
Is not profound; nor will its record be
A chronicle for fame with words that glow
Upon a golden page—except for me.
Should kindred eyes that venture here recall,
As they explore, that we have passed this way,
It is return enough; for, after all,
That prompted me, and not what I would say.

Affinity accepts us as we are;
This voluntary bond, which makes us kin,
Awaits no holiday with shining Star
To open wide the door and take us in.
Ask little else to cheer this interim—
The cup is full if once you reach the brim.

THE END

INDEX

ABC, 93, 139
Ackerley, Bob, 57, 70
"Acres of Clams," 81
"Across Horizons," 64
Adams, Ed, 144-145
"Adventures of Tom and Wash," 169
"Alla Tamanya," 170
American Broadcasting Co., 46-51, 60
American Forces Network, 80
American Marconi Co., 26
American Tel. & Tel. Co., 19, 45
"Amos 'n' Andy," 9, 55, 169
Anderson, Emmett, 115
Anderson, Frank, 86
Anderson, R. H. "Andy," 178, 180-181
Anderson, Warren, 40, 42
"Andy and Sport," 148
Antique Wireless Assn., 188
Apple, Bill, 141-142
Apple, Lois, 142
"Arizona Joe," 86
"Army Hour," 68, 78
Arndt, Bill, 86
"Around the Sound," 81
"Around the World Press Conference," 176
"Aunt Vivian," 9, 34-35, 37-38
Aylesworth, Merlin, 45

Baker, Norman, 124-125
Barber, "Red," 152
Barduhn, Art, 98-99
Barron, Cecile, 48
Bean, Tom, 162
Beardsley, Len, 78, 139-140
Beckley, Leo, 142-143
Beckman, Roy, 30
Belcher, Rod, 164-165
Bell, Alexander Graham, 15
Bell, Ted, 60, 67, 91-92, 94, 144, 162-163, 165
Bellingham Herald, 112, 172-174
Bennett, Stan, 127
Benny, Jack, 12
Benum, Arnold, 120
Berry, Bob, 80
Bevilacqua, Don, 30
"Bill Hatch," 169
Blethen, Alden, 174
Block, Martin, 135
Bloomquist, Rev. Ernest, 31
Blue network, 55, 58, 61, 118
Boggs, Murray, 80
Bone, Homer, 72
Boor, John, 185
Boreson, Stan, 8-9, 98-99, 105, 150, 187
Bowen, Judge John, 174
Bowes, "Major" Edward, 116-118
Bowles, Al, 140
"Brakeman Bill," 9, 13, 130-132
Bras, Ricky, 133
Brashen, Abe, 61
Breneman, Tom, 169
Brinkley, David, 72
Brockman, Syd, 112
Brott, Francis, 89, 127, 168
Brown, Elliott, 105-106, 109
Brown, Neil, 169
Brown, Warren, 138
Brubaker, Bill, 14
Bryan, William Jennings, 31

Bryant, Ted, 124
Bullitt, Dorothy, 94-96, 146
Bullitt, Stimson, 94
Burdick, Hal, 57, 59
Burns, Tommy, 115
Butler, Arthur, 86
Butler Cafe, 36

Calhoun, Bruce, 74-75, 80, 96, 144-146
"Captain Dobbsie," 82-83
"Captain Puget, " 11, 128
Carlson, Stan, 93, 99
Carpenter, Jack, 34
Carpenter, Peg, 124
Caruso, Enrico, 21
Castle, Walter, 54
CBS, 10, 45, 52, 56, 67, 73, 76-77, 86, 93, 116, 119, 128, 133, 148, 161, 176, 188
Cecil, Winifred, 54
Chamberlin, Art, 58, 151
Chandler, Gloria, 106-107
"Cherokee Jack," 120
Chevigny, Hector, 62-65
Clark, "Tubby," 71
Clarke, Jack, 174
Clifford, Eddie, 71
"Clifford and Clark," 71
Clinton, Mayor Gordon, 144
Cody, Wayne, 167, 188
Coghlin, Willard, 58
Concie, Bob, 179
Conrad, Dr. Frank, 23-24
"Cookbook Quiz," 129
Coolidge, Pres. Calvin, 45
Cooney, Lloyd, 148
Corcoran, Bill, 96, 100
Corcoran, Cheri, 100
Cornish School, 62, 64
Correll, Charles, 55
Coscarart, "Coffee Joe," 163
"Cowboy Joe," 84
"Crazy Donkey," 130-131
Crescent Ballroom, 142
Crockett, Dave, 99
Crosby, Bing, 2-3, 10, 52, 64, 84
"Crow's Nest," 144
Cummings, Al, 180, 186

Dailey, Art, 159
Daley, John, 101
"Dandy Time," 130
Dargan, Tom, 96-99
Darst, W. Delbert, 170
Darwin, Leslie H., 173-174
De Forest, Lee, 10, 19, 20, 21, 23
Dempsey-Carpentier fight, 26-27, 151
Dennis, Orville, 126
Denny Hall, 144
Dill, Sen. C. C., 174
Dillon, Harold, 91
Ditmars, Ivan, 64, 66, 86
Dixon, Sydney, 45
Dobbs, Hugh Barrett, 83
Doernbecher, E. M., 116, 119
Don Lee network, 45, 73, 116, 133
"Doña Mercedes," 147
Donovan, Bea, 110-111
Douglas, Justice Wm. O., 75-76
"Dragnet," 66-67
Drysdale, Sharon, 176
Dubilier, William, 18-19

Dubuque, John, 136-138, 140
Duff, Howard, 58, 62, 67, 81
Du Mont network, 93
Dunn, Irene, 54

Eaton, Glen, 86
Ebey, Wesley, 85
Edelson, Howard, 68
Edgerton, Olga Castaneda de, 147
Edison Technical School, 39, 146
Eisenhower, Maj. John, 103
Emel, Alice, 74
"Empire Builders," 64
Evans, Trevor, 66-67, 72, 81, 129
"Exploration Northwest," 128

Fageol, Lou, 166
Farmer, Frances, 64
Fay, Haines, 179
Ferguson, Bob, 93
Ferris, Bob, 70
Fessenden, Reginald, 15, 18-19
"First Nighter," 62
First Presbyterian Church, Seattle, 27, 29, 33, 187
Fisher, Birt, 40-41, 43
Fisher, Dan R., 41
Fisher, Ken, 43-44, 151
Fisher, Oliver David, 40, 41, 43, 45, 56, 186
Fisher, Oliver Williams, 40
Fisher, Orin Wallace, 41
Fisher, Will, 41, 44
Fisher's Blend Station, 41-44, 56, 126
Flora, Dr. Charles "Jerry," 181
Flynn, Bernadine, 12
Forbes, Alex, 86
Ford, Tennessee Ernie, 140
Foster, Nick, 34, 36-39, 134, 146
Fratt, Ruth, see Katherine Wise
Freeman, George, 93
French, Jim, 180
"Friendly Trail," 139-140
Fuhrmeister, Dinwiddie, 130

Garthright, "Hap," 157-160, 162
Garthright, Marie, 160
Gavin, Bill, 82
Gaylord Broadcasting Co., 183
Geehan, Jerry, 126
General Electric Co., 26, 45
Gerald, Bill, 150
Gilmore, Art, 66, 67
Givins, Shirley, 100
Gleason, Bob, 124-125, 130-131
Goddard, Fred, 170
Godfrey, Donald, 188
Gosden, Freeman, 55
Grant, Fred, 143
Gray, Earl, 36-37, 39
Gray, Elisha, 15
Gray, G. Donald, 45
Greco, Helen, 86
Gregarson, Casey, 13, 111
Griffith, Tom, 68
Guinan, "Texas," 27
Guthrie, Jack, 120
Guyman, Bill, 129

Haas, Saul, 72-76, 116, 148, 170, 186
Hackett, Paul J., 19, 20
Haglund, Ivar, 81, 128

Hagman, Leif and Agnes, 116
Hale, Alan, see Al Schuss
Hall, Howard, 111
Hallowell, Lola, 87, 149
Hamstreet, Jim, 179
Hanawalt, Clare, 93, 99
Hanson, John, 31
Harper, Ernie, 174, 177-178, 180
"Harper's Corners," 49
Harris, Dave, 64-65
Harris, Stanley, 64
Harvey, Art Van, 12
Hayes, Pat, 165
Hayes, Sam, 72
Haymond, Carl, 27, 112-116, 126, 128, 151, 168
Haymond, Margaret, 113, 115
Hearst, William Randolph, 74-75
Heerwald, Marty, 143
Hemingway, Jack, 146
Henley, Lewis, see "Cherokee Jack"
Henrickson, Ella, 147
Herbert, Tom, 143-144
Herring, Charles, 103-104
Herrold, Charles "Doc," 21
Hertz, Heinrich, 15
Hesketh, Robert, 154
Heverly, John, 57
Hicks, George, 118
Higgins, Harry, 112
Higgins, Len, 116, 125
Hill, Helene, 86
Hill, Steven, 81
Hoeck, Jerry, 129
Hohler, Herbert, 54
Hoover, Herbert, 33
"How Come?" 129
Hubbard, Al, 33-34, 37, 39, 112-113, 168
Hubbard, Irene, 54
Hughes, Rod, see Rod Belcher
Hull, Alexander Sr., 91
Huntley, Chet, 72
Hurd, Bob, 82
Husing, Ted, 160-161

"I Love Lucy," 129
Idelson, William, 12
International Good Music, 180, 184
Isham, Don, 64

"J. P. Patches," 9, 11, 148-150
"Jack Armstrong," 64
James, Burton, 49
Jamieson, "Jamie," 81
Jansen, Eddie, 119
Jarstad, John, 165
Johnson, Lyndon, 76
Jones, Casey, 61
Jones, Rogan, 168-180
Jordan, Harry, 122
Jorgenson, Oscar Marcos, 84-85
"Junior G-Men," 67, 81

Kager, Ken, 145-146
KAYO, 91, 136
KBAY, 180
KBRC, 142-143
KCPQ, 128
KCTS, 39, 75, 146-147, 185
KDKA, 23
KDZE, 32-33
KDZR, 173
Keef, Robert, 49
Kenyon, Dr. Essek, 116

Keplinger, Dick, 68-70, 78, 129
Kessler, Louis, 169-170, 173
KEVR, 94-95
KEX, 46
KFBL, 142, 187
KFC, 27, 31, 33, 92, 112, 187
KFIO, 136
KFMU, 180
KFMW, 180
KFOA, 44-45, 82, 112, 137, 151
KFQW, 134
KFQX, 33-40, 43, 95, 169
KGA, 46
KGB, 31-32, 112, 115, 187
KGBU, 112-113
KGFA, 43
KGMB, 180
KGMI, 178-180
KGMJ, 180
KGW, 72
KGY, 28, 133, 187
KHQ, 32-33, 72
KING (radio), 95-96, 122, 146, 165
KING-TV, 13, 95-111, 164-166
King, Bruce, 14
King, Jan, 137
King, Jean Paul, 118-119
King Broadcasting Co., 94-111
"King's Clubhouse," 105
"King's Queen," 110
KIRO (radio), 71-81, 85-86, 116, 137, 167, 180, 188
KIRO-TV, 11, 122, 130, 148-150, 167
KISW, 146
KJR, 9, 24-25, 33, 45-62, 64, 66-70, 72, 75, 81, 84, 116, 152-154, 160, 187
Klepper, Bill, 154-155
KMO (radio), 31, 112-116, 120-123
KMO-TV, 126, 128
KOL, 45, 64, 66-67, 73, 86, 116, 119, 133
"KOL Carnival," 86
Kolesar, J. D., 115
KOMO (radio), 42-46, 54, 56-59, 62, 64, 66-68, 72, 81-83, 88, 167-168, 188
KOMO-TV, 14, 42, 89, 94, 126-129
Koons, Bob, 101
KPCB, 71-73, 168-170
KPO, 83
KPQ, 168, 170, 175
Kraft, Ed, 134
Kraft, Vincent, 24-25, 27, 40-41, 46, 89, 116, 134, 157, 180, 186-187
Krakovski, Saul, see Steven Hill
KRKO, 142, 162, 187
KRSC (radio), 89-92, 96, 136, 142, 160, 162-163
KRSC-TV, 90-96, 164, 174
KSTW, 148, 183
KTAC, 119
KTBI, 119
KTCL, 40-43
KTNT (radio), 124-125
KTNT-TV, 124-132, 148, 177, 183
KTW, 29-30, 33, 187
KUOW, 75, 146
KVI, 66, 73, 116, 119, 130, 134, 148
KVL, 158-159
KVOS (radio), 168-174, 178-180
KVOS-TV, 126, 174-181
KVOS TV-Cable, 174
KWSC, 76, 123
KXA, 43, 84, 130, 134-141, 148, 157, 186
KXLE, 178
KXRO, 168, 170

KYA, 46
KZC, 32-33

Langlie, Gov. Arthur, 127
Larsen, Norma, see Norma Zimmer
Lassen, Leo, 9, 154-165, 167, 188
Lassen, Minnie, 154-155, 160, 164, 167
Latham, Jack, 135-137
Laurie, Piper, 123
Leberman, Palmer, 89-90, 94, 186
Leese, Otto, and Bob, 142, 187
Leonard, Elizabeth, 13, 111
Levienne, Kolia, 48
Lewis, Jim, see "Sheriff Tex"
Lewis, Joe, 152
Lindbergh, Charles, 43, 45
Linden, Adolph, 46, 48-51
Linkletter, Art, 88
Lippincott, Ellwood, 146
"Little Tyke," 108-109
Livingstone, Mary, 12
"Lone Ranger," 68, 73, 187
Long, Harry Russell, 119
Longo, Francesco, 47
Love Electric Co., 112
Lowe, Billy, 86
Luke, Anna, 30
Lunceford, Jimmy, 137
Lyle, Roy, 37-38

Malbin, Irene, 111
"March of Time," 68-69
"March On," 99, 101
Marconi, Guglielmo, 15-18, 26, 89
"Mardi Gras," 60-61
Marks, Sadie, see Mary Livingstone
"Mary's Friendly Garden," 60
Marzano, Roy, 30
Matthews, Rev. Mark, 29
McCarthy, Clem, 162
McCarthy, Sen. Joseph, 104
McCloy, Ruth, 88
McCoy, Bob, 140
McCrea, Paul, 86
McCune, Don, 128, 150
McDonald, Betty, 130, 145
McIntyre, Frank, 54
McLain, Bill, 13, 130-132
McNamee, Graham, 31, 45
McQuade, Don, 64
Meggee, Roland, 134
Mentrin, Charles, 100
"Merceedes," 104
Merenblum, Peter, 48
Merrill, Grant, 60
Meyer, Ken, 137
Meyers, Vic, 53-54
Miller, Al, 99
Miller, Clarence "Doc," 142
Milligan, Don, 58
Mintz, Dave, 177-180
"Miss Colorvision," 127, 129
"Mission Impossible," 81
Morgenthau, Henry, 75
Morris, Charles, 122
Morris, Paul, 91, 93
Morse, Jane, see Margaret Haymond
Morse, Samuel F. B., 15
Mount Constitution, 176-177
"Mr. Wyde-Awake," 62-63, 80
Mudge, Bill, 150
Mudgett, Lee, 91
Mullins Electric Co., 112
Mundt, Sen. Carl, 104

Murphy, H. Ben, 171
Murrow, Ed, 11, 76-78
Mutual network, 73, 116, 119

NBC, 27, 44-45, 54-57, 61, 72, 93, 119, 128
Neidigh, Jim, 136-137, 139
Nelson, Lindsay, 165
Neterer, Judge Nehemiah, 168
Newman, Bob, 11
"Newspaper of the Air," 173-174
Nichols, Bob, 27, 54, 87, 151, 153
"Night Editor," 57, 59
Niles, Ken, 67
Niles, Wendell, 66-67, 71, 86
Nipkow, Paul, 89
"No Mo Shun," 105
Northwest Broadcasting System, 53, 55

Olmstead, Elise "Elsie," 33-39
Olmstead, Roy, 33-40, 43, 95, 112-113, 134, 157, 168-169
O'Mara, Bill, 94, 96, 163-164
"Oofty and Goofty," 170
Orange network, 45
"Original Amateur Hour," 116-117
Ottenheimer, Al, 31, 49, 62-63
"Our State at War," 81
Owens, Buck, 120

Pacific Coast Biscuit Co., 71, 73
Pacific Coast Network, 45, 61
Page, Connie, 124, 130
Paley, William, 10, 56, 116, 161
Parsons, Ed, 174
Patterson, Fred, 62
Pearson, John, 49, 62-63
Peckham, George, 85, 144
Pierce, Ahira, 50, 53-54, 72
"Pioneers," 62-65, 67
Poore, Hugh, 84
Popov, Alexander, 15
Price, Carol, 127
Priebe, Bob, 91, 93
Priebe, Tom, 92, 96, 99
Prins, Ruth, 9-10, 106-110, 144
Puget Sound Savings & Loan, 51
Puget Sound Wireless Assn., 188

Queen City Broadcasting Co., 170
"Quicksilver," 164
Quilliam, Harold, 151
Racine, Ed, 103
Radio City, 55
"Radio Gospel League," 116
Radio Hall, 144-146
Ramsay, Ray, 14
RCA, 26-27, 45, 92
"Reading for Fun," 144-145
Reagan, Ronald, 157
Red network, 55, 58
Redington, Bernice, 58
Reed, Warren, 130-131
Reichert, Howard, 112
Reilly, Earl, 139-140
Reuter, Bill, 73
Reuther, "Dutch," 160
Rhodes, Bill, see Bill O'Mara
Rhodes, Mike, 111
Rhodes Bros. Department Stores, 32, 44, 112, 116, 137, 139-140, 151
Rhymer, Paul, 12
Richardson, David, 132, 138
"Richfield Reporter," 72
Rifkin, George, 91

Ritchie, Buck, 119
Roberts, Al, 145-146
Rogstad, Tom, 99
Roosevelt, Pres. Franklin D., 11, 26, 62, 68, 72-73, 90, 168, 174
Ross, James D., 27, 29, 187
Ross, James S., 30
Ross, Lanny, 54, 84
Rothafel, Sam "Roxy," 118, 162
Rowan, Mark, 86
"Roxy's Gang," 118
Rue, Walter, 58
Ruth, Babe, 27
Ruth, Father Sebastian, 23, 27-28, 187
"Ruth and Dick," 88
Ryan, Milo, 147

"Sam Spade," 67
Sanislo, Stephen, 82
Sarnoff, David, 26-27, 44-45, 55
Satellite TV, 182-183, 185
Sawin, Paul, 99
"Scandinavian Reporter," 84-85
Schipa, Tito, 46
Schonely, Bill, 144
Schulman, Lee, 90, 92, 96, 98-100, 106
Schuss, Al, 61, 75, 151-152
Seattle P-I, 26, 31, 44, 52, 57-58, 75, 90, 92-93, 112, 151, 153, 155, 160, 173-174, 187
Seattle Star, 55, 155-156, 158
"Seattle Streets," 64
Seattle Times, 57, 59, 68, 173-174
Sefrit, Frank Ira, 173-174
"Senator Fishface," 60-61
Setterberg, Doug, 187
Sevareid, Eric, 112
Shaw, Stan, 135
Shawcroft, Jack, 92-93
Shepard, Jack, 126
"Sheriff Tex," 11, 102
Sherman, John, 30
Shreeve, Craig, 148
Shults, Alex, 155, 159-160
Sills, Beverly, 118
Sivertson, Borghild, 31
Skelton, Red, 66
Slo-Mo-Shun V, 166
Smith, Al, 102, 110, 166
Smith, Thomas Freebairn, 50-51
Smith, Wheeler, 86
"So Goes the World," 63, 68-69, 71
Sohl, Marshall, 61
Solly, Cecil, 81-82
Spence, Harry, 168-170
"Spike Hogan," 139-140
"Spook Club," 137
Spurling, Mac, 112
Starrett, Mary, 181
"Stay-Up Stan," 135-137, 139, 141
Stenso, Alvin, 30-31, 112, 115
Stenso, Esther, 31
Stern, Bill, 160, 162
Stevens, Bill, 108
Stevens, Jim, 50
Stewart, Al, 30
Stuart, Ken Jr., 152
Stuart, Ken Sr., 66, 86, 152, 154
Stubblefield, Bernard, 16-17
Stubblefield, Nathan, 15-18
"Sunshine and Sparky," 58
Sutherland, Mitchell, 49
Swanson, Gloria, 99
Swift, Al, 178-179

Swisher, Ben, 93

Tacoma Ledger, 112, 187
Tacoma News Tribune, 124
Taft, Archie, 116, 133
Talbot, Arch, 94-95
Talcott, Mique, 93, 99
"Telaventure Tales," 106-107
Thomas, Lowell, 73
Thoms, Earl, 133, 139, 157-158, 166
Thomsen, Moritz, 71-72, 168
Thorne, Gordon, 147
Titanic, S. S., 26
Tost, Lou, 163
Totem Broadcasters, 43-44
Tovey, Frank, 31
Towey, Joe, 11
Tubesing, Gary, 147
Tuell, Gordon, 80
"Two B's at the Keys," 98-99

University of Washington, 19, 75, 126, 143-147, 151, 188

"Vagabond Baritone," 169
Van Rooy, C. W., 115
Van Voorhis, Westbrook, 69
"Vic and Sade," 12, 188
Vincent, Elmore, 60-61
"Vintage Radio," 188
"Visible telephone," 5, 89

WABC, 135
Wacker, Phil, 85
Walker, Sally Jo, 45, 61
Wallace, Al, 129
Wallenstein, Alfred, 180
Wallis, Hal, 85
Warren, Willard "Bill," 127
Washington State College, 76
Wasmer, Louis, 32
Watertown, S. S., 95
Webb, Jack, 67
Wedes, Chris, 11, 148-150
Weeks, Dick, 123
Welk, Lawrence, 99, 121
Weller, Velva, 60
Welles, Orson, 62
Wertz, Hoyt, 176
WGY, 62, 89
White, J. Andrew, 161
Whitney, Bill, 37, 39
Wienand, Mark, 44
Wilson, Doc, 58
Winder, Bill, 113
Wise, Katherine, 129
WJZ, 135
WNEW, 135
"Women in Defense," 74
Wometco Enterprises, 177
WOR, 73
WTVJ, 177
"Wunda Wunda," see Ruth Prins
WWJ, 21

Zimmer, Norma, 121

7AD, 127
7XC, 24-25, 187
7XV, 31, 112
7XZ, 143
7YS, 23, 28, 187
8MK, 21
8XK, 23